BUSINESS ACQUISITION PRINCIPLES

EVERYTHING YOU NEED TO KNOW

DR GAJANAN SHIRKE

Made with ♥ on the Notion Press Platform
www.notionpress.com

I would like to express a special debt of gratitude to my wife Rajeshree and my two daughters Rupeshi & Kavya, for their support and guidancel would like to express a special debt of gratitude to my wife Rajeshree and my two daughters Rupeshi & Kavya.

Contents

Preface *vii*

Index *ix*

About Author *xi*

1. Basic Corporate Documents And Documents For Any Subsidiary 1
2. Securities Issuances 17
3. Financial Matters 22
4. Licenses And Permits 34
5. Shareholder Information 37
6. Material Contracts 39
7. Patent And Trademark Matters 58
8. Manufacturing / Operational Aspects 60
9. Operations 67
10. Sales And Marketing 69
11. Tangible Property 72
12. Litigation And Audits 73
13. Environmental 77
14. Employees 79
15. Management 81
16. Other Review 83

Preface

About Book

Progression through acquisition is quicker, cheaper, and far less risky than more traditional methods of growing a company. Business acquisition principles shows how small and midsize companies can expand by acquisition, and the incredible advantages of doing so. This book covers all the steps from finding acquisition targets to evaluating and valuing potential acquisitions, to financing, negotiating, and finalizing a deal.

Index

1. Basic Corporate Documents and Documents for Any Subsidiary
2. Securities Issuances
3. Financial Matters
4. Licenses and Permits
5. Shareholder Information
6. Material Contracts
7. Patent and Trademark Matters
8. Manufacturing / Operational Aspects
9. Operations
10. Sales and Marketing
11. Tangible Property
12. Litigation and Audits
13. Environmental
14. Employees
15. Management
16. Other Review

About Author

About the Author

Gajanan Shirke, a hotel consultant, has years of extensive experience in the hospitality industry. His thirst for learning and aspiration to become a multi-faceted expert in the hotel industry helped him rise from employment to becoming an independent professional in the hospitality sector. Since his last assignment as General Manager at Kamat Hotels, he has become a renowned hotel consultant with a proven track record of developing, training and growing some of the best-known hotels, restaurants and fast-food joints in the Indian market. He was appointed as an expert consultant for The Eighth meeting of the Board of Studies for Hotel Management & Catering Technology. He is a visiting faculty at various Hotel Management Colleges and has trained over a thousand hospitality professionals. He has completed numerous pre and post opening hotel consultancies in India and overseas.

In order to spread his extensive knowledge to aspiring hotel professionals, Gajanan has penned a large number of books spanning different segments of the hospitality industry. Starting from his first book 'Bar Management and Operations' published in 2010, he has written 48 books including Hospitality Management, Food and Beverage Management, Hotel Engineering Management, Front Office Management, Hotel Housekeeping Management, The Cookery Trilogy: Advance Cookery Theory, The Cookery Trilogy: Foundation of Cookery, The Cookery Trilogy: The Basic Cookery Book, Hotel Sales and Marketing, Hospitality Industry Accounting & Fundamentals, Customer Interaction Excellence in Hospitality, History of Indian Cuisine – Volume 1, History of Indian Cuisine – Volume 2, Hotel Owner's Manual, Hotel Security & Prevention, Training Manager's Manual, Exceptional Service In Hospitality Six Sigma Way, etc

CHAPTER ONE

Basic Corporate Documents and Documents for Any Subsidiary

A subsidiary is a separate legal business entity that generates its own revenue and debt, but remains under the control of the "parent" company. Companies often form subsidiaries in order to exploit new business opportunities in the hopes of enhancing the position of the parent company, while not exposing the parent company to risk. To limit risk to the parent company and its shareholders, the subsidiary must legally incorporate as a corporation or a limited liability company. To do this the subsidiary must draft bylaws and articles of incorporation (for corporations) or articles of organization (for LLCs).

Checklist Documents to check

a. **Articles of Incorporation and By-laws**

Articles of incorporation contain all the company's establishment and background details. They are to be prepared as per the requirement specified by the government while creating a new company. Such documents are verified by the government and contain particulars of the corporate's legal existence. They are to be kept in a permanent file to remain available, if required, during the audit.

What must be included in the articles of incorporation?: Each state has somewhat different requirements regarding what must be included in the articles of incorporation. Typically, the articles must contain, at the very least:

- the corporation's name and business address
- the number of authorized shares and the par value (if any) of the shares
- the name and address of the in-state
- the names and addresses of its incorporators

If there will be more than one class of shares, the articles must include the number of authorized shares of each class and a description of the rights of each class. Some states require that the articles of incorporation include additional information, such as:

- the corporation's purpose (which can be a general statement such "to engage in all purposes permitted by law")
- the number of the initial directors
- the names and addresses of the initial directors.
- its duration, if not perpetual

The articles of incorporation may be thought of as the "birth certificate" of a corporation. In most cases, only basic information is required. However, it is important to remember that statutory requirements, such as what form to use, where to file, what fees to pay and to whom, etc., vary greatly from state to state. And, in many cases, the parties will want to customize the articles to override statutory default provisions. For these reasons, it's important to work with compliance experts who are aware of the nuances of each state's requirements and can help their customers with these requirements.

a. **Minutes of all meetings of directors, committees of directors, and shareholders:**

Minutes means a formal written record, in physical or electronic form, of the proceedings of a Meeting and Minutes Book means a Book maintained in physical or in electronic form for the purpose of recording of Minutes. Every company shall cause minutes of the proceedings of every general meeting of any class of shareholders or creditors, and every resolution passed by postal ballot and every meeting of its Board of Directors or of every committee of the Board, to be prepared and signed in such manner as may be prescribed and kept within 30 days of the conclusion of every such meeting concerned, or passing of resolution by postal ballot in books kept for that purpose with their pages consecutively numbered.

A distinct minute book shall be maintained for each type of meeting namely

1. General Meetings of the Members
2. Board Meeting of the Directors
3. Meetings of each Committee of the Board
4. Meetings of the Creditors

Resolutions passed by postal ballot shall be recorded in the minute book of general meetings as if it has been deemed to be passed in the general meeting.

INFORMATION CONTAINED IN THE MINUTES:

General Content	Specific Content
Serial Number of the Meeting Type of Meeting Name of the Company Date and Time of the Meeting Venue of the Meeting Conclusion time of the meeting Attendance of the directors Name of the directors physically present Name of the Directors present through electronic mode Company secretary of the Company Special Invitee (if any)	Election of Chairman of the Meeting Granting Leave of absence of director Mode of Attendance of directors Ascertainment of quorum Confirmation of minutes of preceding meeting Noting of Resolution passed by circulation (if any) Any other item for which meeting was convened

Enter Caption

INSPECTION AND EXTRACTS OF MINUTES: Directors, Company secretary, Secretarial Auditor, Statutory Auditor, Cost Auditor, Internal Auditor can inspect the minutes. However, the members of the company are not entitled to inspect minutes. Extracts of the minutes of the meeting can be given only to the director of the company.

Disclaimer: –The above mentioned article has been based on relevant provisions of Companies Act, 2013 . Under no circumstance, the author shall not liable for any direct, indirect, special or incidental damage resulting from, arising out of or in connection with the use of the information.

a. **List of all states and/or countries where property owned or leased or where employees are located, indicating in which states the Company is qualified to do business**

Look at factors to determine whether the business is localized to the extent that qualification is necessary. These include the following:

- Does company have a physical presence (like a factory or stores) in other state?
- Does company have employees in the other state?
- Does company accept orders in the other state, or have liability to collect sales tax?

Be aware that this is not a complete list.

The most serious consequence is that states deny non-compliant companies the right to bring or maintain a lawsuit or other legal proceeding in their court system. This means that a company wouldn't be able to sue to recover damages or to enforce a contract

Financial risk: Another costly consequence to failing to qualify if business entity meets the state's registration criteria is that states will assess fines, penalties and back taxes for the time the company was/is transacting business without obtaining a certificate of authority to do so.

a. **Samples of common and preferred stock certificates, warrants, options, debentures, and any other outstanding securities**

Stock Warrants vs. Stock Options: An Overview

A stock warrant gives the holder the right to purchase a company's stock at a specific price and at a specific date. A stock warrant is issued directly by the company concerned; when an investor exercises a stock warrant, the shares that fulfill the obligation are not received from another investor but directly from the company.

An equity stock option, on the other hand, is a contract between two people that gives the holder the right, but not the obligation, to buy or sell a stock at a specific price, prior to a specific date, referred to as the contract expiration date.

- A stock warrant represents the right to purchase a company's stock at a specific price and at a specific date.
- A stock warrant is issued directly by a company to an investor.
- Stock options are purchased when it is believed the price of a stock will go up or down.
- Stock options are typically traded between investors.
- A stock warrant represents future capital for a company.

Before you decide to invest in a company, you should find out what types of financings the company has engaged in - including convertible security deals - and make sure that you understand the effects those financings might have on the company and the value of its securities. Even if the company sells convertible securities in a private, unregistered transaction (or "private placement"), the company and the purchaser normally agree that the company will register the underlying common stock for the purchaser's resale prior to conversion. You'll also find disclosures about these and other financings in the company's annual and quarterly reports that announce the financing transaction. If the company has engaged in convertible security financings, be sure to ascertain the nature of the convertible financing arrangement - fixed versus market price based conversion ratios. Be sure you fully understand the terms of the convertible security financing arrangement, including the circumstances of its issuance and how the conversion formula works. You should also understand the risks and the possible effects on the company and its outstanding securities arising from the below market price conversions and potentially significant additional share issuances and sales, including dilution to shareholders. You should be aware of the risks arising from the effects of the purchasers and other parties trading strategies, such as short selling activities, on the market price for the company's securities, which may affect the amount of shares issued on future conversions.

c. **Bank Statements**

Even if you and your bank record everything correctly, your ledger and the bank statement may not match. Deposits and checks don't always clear before your statement goes out. Reconciling the bank statement can correct for that, but reconciliation can go wrong too. The next level of correction is to audit the bank account.

Reconciling your bank statement is less rigorous and demanding than an audit, but it's based on the same principle: You need to know how much cash you have on hand. Reconciliation is a way to spot errors, both yours and the bank's. If you pay for a professional audit, the auditor is going to want a reconciliation statement before they audit the bank account. Suppose you've just received your March statement from the bank, listing deposits, checks, withdrawals and service charges. Sit down with the statement and your accounting journal and go over them in detail. If there are inconsistencies, note them on the reconciliation statement. For example, if you wrote a 1,500 check on March 29 and it hadn't cleared the bank when the statement went out, you note the difference on the reconciliation statement. When you finish reconciliation, you should have an explanation for every difference between the figures on the bank statement and the figures in your ledger.

CHECKLIST FOR AN IN-HOUSE BANK RECONCILIATION AUDIT

1. Gather your bank statement, general ledger, and bank reconciliation documents for the month you're auditing.
2. Compare the final figures on your reconciliation document to that account's bank statement. The amounts should match.
3. Check the final figures on your bank reconciliation document against your general ledger totals and ensure they match.
4. Calculate the difference between your bank statement ending balance and your general ledger total. Your bank statement should properly reflect the difference.
5. Match transactions from your bank statement and general ledger account. Each transaction in one document should have a corresponding transaction in the other. To avoid confusion, mark these off as you go.
6. Highlight any non-matching transactions between your general ledger and bank statement. These items are 'reconciling' and should be accounted for in your bank reconciliation document with a full explanation for the discrepancy. These items are usually the result of funds that have not yet cleared or checks that are waiting to be cleared.
7. Double-check that the difference between your bank statement and general ledger is properly accounted for.

d. **Intellectual properties registration documents**

Intellectual property is a legal term for the creations of mind and intellectual property rights are the rights provided by law for the exclusive use of creations of the mind. Examples of intellectual property include music, literature, and other artistic works; discoveries and inventions; and words, phrases, symbols, and designs. Examples of intellectual property rights include trademark, copyright and patent. In this article, we look at intellectual property rights available in India. Infringement is the most commonly occurring intellectual property dispute in India. Intellectual property is a non-physical asset that has a set of rights to regulate who owns the asset, including creative work, academic work, names and images, developments, logos, and other items used to grow a business. Registration procedure for an Intellectual Property in India is easy.

Intellectual Property Rights Registration: In India, the intellectual property rights pertaining to trademarks and patents are controlled by the Controller General of Patents Designs and Trademarks, Department of Industrial Policy and Promotion, Ministry of Commerce and Industry. Copyrights are handled by the Copyright Office, Copyright Societies, Government of India. Based on the type of intellectual property right to be registered, application must be made to the concerned authorities in the prescribed form.

Different types of Intellectual Property

- Trademark: Trademark works as a symbol which helps in recognizing the merchandise and services of one undertaking from the other endeavour.
- Industrial Designs: An industrial design discusses the elaborate and stylish detailing in an article. Design is a three- dimensional feature for example shapes or surface of an article or it tends to be a two-dimensional feature such as shading, design, lines.
- Copyright: A legally defined term which portrays the rights that any maker or innovator holds over their creation and advancement. Copyright covers different works for example music, films, sculpture, promotion, maps, artworks, books, computer programs and technical drawings.
- Geographical Indication: Geographical indication and assignments of the source are signs used on merchandise that have a specific land root and have attributes, reputation or qualities that are fundamentally inferable from that place of origin.

- Patent: The patent is an exceptional right given to the proprietor of the maker. A patent gives the proprietor an option to choose what he/she needs to do with the innovation which can be utilized by others. As an end-result of this right, the patent owner makes particular information relating to the innovation freely accessible in the appropriated patent document.
- Trade Secrets: Trade secrets are only Intellectual Property rights which intend to ensure confidential information. In any occasion of unapproved securing or disclosure of confidential information falls under uncalled for training and encroachment of trade secret protection.

Types of Intellectual Property Disputes

Infringement is considered as the most common type of intellectual property dispute. Infringement occurs when someone dares to use the intellectual property without legally asking the owner of the property.

Thus, There Can Be:

- Copyright infringement
- Patent infringement
- Trademark infringement

Following Cases Can Be Named As Infringement:

- Making copies of musical recordings, films, and other media and passing on them for advantage without the copyright owner's assent.
- Assembling a patented thing by following the portrayal recorded in the patent without having a permit from the patent proprietor.
- Utilizing the logo for one item on another result of a comparative sort as the principal item.
- Making a logo or using an exchange dress is a way that is wanted to make purchasers think they are purchasing an item that is proportionate to the first item.
- Intellectual Property Dispute can likewise emerge out of misconception or because of the carelessness of the proprietor of the property. In the event when the proprietor accepts that their item is made sure about under Intellectual Property laws rather than the real world, the surface proprietor overlooks or neglects to make sure about the item under Intellectual Property law.

Intellectual Property Rights

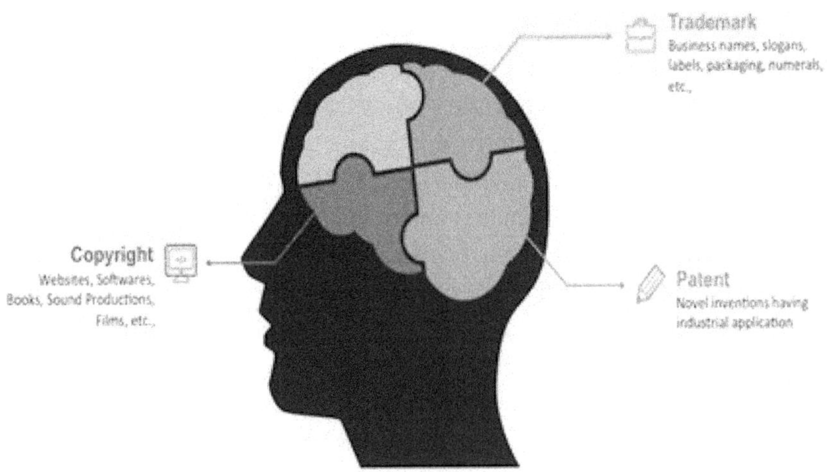

Enter Caption

a. **Copies of:**

- Any voting trust, shareholder, or other similar agreement covering any portion of the Company's shares
- All agreements relating to repurchases, redemptions, exchanges, conversions, or similar transactions
- All agreements containing registration rights or assigning such rights and preemptive rights or assigning such rights
- Stock books of the company
- All quarterly and annual reports and any other communications to the company's shareholders within the past five years
- All press releases issued by the company within the past five years.
- List of all subsidiaries

a. **Legal due diligence for all real estate properties of the company.**

A due diligence exercise is probably the most important aspect of a transaction involving real estate immediately following a broad understanding of the commercials. This process has the potential of not only impacting the commercials but also determining the feasibility of the transaction itself. While the commercials often pay high importance to expedite the conclusion of a transaction, it is critical in the interests of the players to provide adequate time and attention to a detailed due diligence of the property involved. It is important to realize issues such as title, permitted use, legality of construction, encumbrances and easements which have the ability to impact the very nature of the property and its suitability to the commercial needs of the transaction.

Scope of legal due diligence of real property:

Due diligence is conducted mainly to verify the ownership of title over the property and any encumbrances over the property, so as to protect one against pre-existing claims over the property. Such claims could either effect the ability of the transferor to transfer the property or could attach themselves to the property even after it is transferred.

The primary objective of a due diligence is therefore to gather information. The extent and type of due diligence to be undertaken by the purchaser's lawyer will depend on the following:

i. the risk profile and business objectives of the purchaser/ lessee;
ii. the type of real asset involved;
iii. nature of the real estate transaction (i.e., whether it is a purchase, long term/ short term lease, mortgage or financing of the real property);
iv. the time frame for completion of the transaction; and
v. whether the purchaser is looking at obtaining third party financing either pre-transaction or post-transaction.

In case of a prospective purchase, a lease of the property or real estate financing, a title search is performed primarily to answer three questions:

i. Does the owner/ lessor have sufficient authority/ interest/ right to enter into the transaction involving the property in question?
ii. Do any liens exist on the property which needs to be discharged before the consummation of the transaction in question? These could be in

the nature of mortgages, charges, acquisitions, unpaid taxes, litigation, easements and other assessments.

iii. What are the nature of restrictions on the use of the property?

Apart from undertaking title search/ due diligences for purchase or lease of properties, a title search/ due diligence is also performed when an owner wishes to mortgage the property with any bank, financial institution or a lender. Such bank/ financial institution/ lender may require the owner to submit a due diligence report of the property or may conduct such diligence on its own.

Type of Due Diligence/ Title Search:

Depending upon the nature of the transaction, the property involved and the objective of the participants, a due diligence can be divided into two broad categories:

i. Full search; and
ii. Limited search.

Full Search: A full search is usually done while giving a title certificate of the property in instances of sale/ resale/ long term lease transactions and for transactions that involve obtaining of financing by mortgaging the property in question. In a full search, the search regarding status of ownership of the property is generally conducted for a period preceding thirty (30) years (or more) from the date on which the seller in question came to acquire the property. It also includes a detailed search of all aspects relating to the history of that property such as the status of encumbrances over the property, the status of disputes relating to the property, the applicable regulations and the status of compliance of such applicable regulations relating to the property in question.

Limited Search: A limited search is generally conducted in transactions where the property is taken on lease for a short term (usually under 9 years). In such instances, the period for which the preceding ownership of the property is traced is generally restricted to fifteen (15) years (or less) from the date on which the current owner of the property came to acquire the property. Unlike full searches, in a limited search, the search relating to the history of the property may be limited to restricted aspects such as recent title history, encumbrances on the property, disputes related to the property etc.

Steps involved in conducting such due diligence/ title search:

In order to conduct a title search/ title verification, the following aspects would require to be examined:

i. Legal capacity of the present owner of the property (whether the person is legally capable of entering into a binding contract for sale or lease of the property or for mortgaging the property);
ii. Nature of current owner's right over the property, and whether such right is transferrable;
iii. Source of right or title of the current owner;
iv. Legality of the construction;
v. Encumbrances over the property; and
vi. Whether the property is a part of any acquisition process.

Step 1: Legal capacity of the seller:

It is necessary to ensure whether the current owner of the property or any of the predecessor title holders of such owner is:

a. a minor (a person, who is below 18 years of age); or
b. a person of unsound mind.

In case of minor's land: If the current owner of the property is a minor, then the property can neither be purchased nor be taken on lease without prior permission of competent authorities. Who or what shall be the 'competent authority' will depend upon the personal laws applicable to the minor. For example, in case of a minor who is a Hindu, permission is required to be obtained from the civil courts under applicable sections of the Hindu Minority and Guardianship Act, 1956 before the guardian of the minor can deal with the minor's property in any manner.

In case the owner is a person of unsound mind: Only a person appointed as a guardian, by a competent court under the Mental Health Act, 1987, can sell the property on behalf a person of unsound mind.

Step 2: Nature of current owner's right over the property:

It is necessary to identify the nature of the right that the current owner has over the property and the transferability of such right. The types of rights that an owner can have over the property can be classified as follows:

a. free hold or absolute ownership;

b. right of perpetual lease;
c. tenancy right; and
d. land allotted by State Government/ Central Government under various enactments.

Step 3: Source of right or title of the current owner:

In India, a person can acquire right or title over the property in following ways:

a. by purchase:
   In case the title was acquired by purchase, then one needs to examine the registered[1] sale deed/ conveyance deed along with the title documents of the predecessors' title holders of the property.
b. by inheritance: If the title was acquired by inheritance, the basis of such inheritance would require to be determined, i.e., whether by way of a will or applicable laws of inheritance. It would also require to be determined whether there is any other person(s) who would have a similar claim of inheritance over the property. An understanding of the personal laws would also be required in this analysis. If the owner claims inheritance jointly with other persons, then it should be checked whether there was any partition.
c. by partition: If the current owner has acquired title over the property by way of partition, then one needs to examine the deed of partition to ascertain whether there were any conditions or restrictions in the deed which may affect the enjoyment/ transferability of property.
d. by gift: If the title was acquired by way of gift, then the registered gift deed needs to be examined to check if there are any conditions, like reservation of life interest, restrictions for alienation, payment of maintenance, pre-emption etc.
e. by will: In case, the title has devolved upon the current owner by virtue of a will, it is advisable to examine the will as well as the order passed by the probate court granting probate/ letters of administration of the property, if any.
f. by perpetual lease:If the title was acquired by perpetual lease, then the deed of lease has to be examined to determine the transferability of the right and the conditions to such transfer. The extent of the rights of the lessor should also be examined.

Step 4: Legality of the Construction:

If the property involves a construction on the land, it also becomes necessary to examine the legality of the construction. Each State government (and the relevant local authorities) lay down their own rules and regulations which govern the manner in which civil constructions need to be carried out in that particular State. Therefore, a lawyer, undertaking a due diligence of land having a structure on it, needs to first get familiar with the local construction laws applicable in the region in which the building is situated, and then, to determine whether these have been complied with, in undertaking the construction of the building in question. The aspects which would need to be examined in this process would be the footprint area (including set-backs), the extent of constructed area, the number of units constructed, the height of the construction and such other aspects.

Step 5: Encumbrances over the property:

It is necessary to verify whether there are any encumbrances, charges, or mortgages on the property in question. The records of the concerned Sub-Registrar of Properties should be examined to ensure that the property is free from all sorts of registered encumbrances or charges or mortgages. It is also advisable to obtain an encumbrance certificate issued by the concerned Sub-Registrar of Properties which would detail the registered encumbrances, if any, on the property. This certificate may be obtained from the office of the Sub-Registrar for Properties, where the property is situated.

In addition, since a mortgage could also be created over the property by way of deposit of title deeds, the original title documents of the property should be inspected to ensure absence of such unregistered mortgages. Further, if an encumbrance is created over a property which belongs to a company then such encumbrance needs to be registered with the Registrar of Companies. Therefore, if we are conducting due diligence of a property where the current owner is a company then the records of Registrar of Companies need to be inspected in order to ascertain absence of encumbrance over the property in question. If there is an existing encumbrance, charge or mortgage over the property, it should either be cleared prior to the purchase or provided for in the consideration.

Step 6: Whether the Land is a part of any acquisition process:

It is also important to know if the property is under the process of acquisition by any government authority. If the property has been acquired by the government, then the property ceases to belong to its original owner and becomes the property of the acquiring authority. Thus, the property so acquired cannot be sold or alienated further by the original owner of the said property, unless the property has been released from the acquisition process.

Needs to undertake the following before issuing a title certificate:

- Peruse the title-deeds in original.
- Undertake searches in the offices of the sub-registrar of properties. This search should cover a period of at least the last 30 years. In case of agricultural land, search should also be undertaken at the local patwari/ tehsildar's office. In case of companies, a search of the records of the Registrar of Companies should also be undertaken.
- Obtain an encumbrance certificate.
- Make enquiries on title and obtain satisfactory answers.
- Obtain declarations on oath from the relevant persons regarding the factual position before issuing the certificate of title.
- Public notices should be published in at least two newspapers (one in vernacular and the other in English circulating in the area where the property is situated) inviting claims of members of the public against, or in respect of, the property in question.

c. **No objection from Secured Creditor for transfer of the company.**

Date:

To, ...

....

....

Sub: No objection Certificate for Conversion of Public Company into Private Company.

Dear Sir,

With reference to the captioned subject matter in regard to Conversion of Public Company into Private Company, I/we. .... am/are the Creditor of the Company and as on .... an amount as stated below is due to me/us by the Company.

I/We hereby confirm that I/we have no objection for Conversion of Public Company into Private Company.

Outstanding Amount Rs. ....

Thanking you.

Yours faithfully,
For ....

....

(.................................)

d. Verification of court documents and court filings, if any.

Currently, the court records of Supreme Court and most of the High Courts are available online. Since most of the districts court records are still not available online, physical verification of such records is carried out with the associated courts.

A court record check includes checking for:

- Court judgments.
- Criminal investigations.
- Databases covering terrorists.
- Most wanted criminals
- Members of parties
- Groups that are on watch
- Financial frauds
- Misconduct

CHAPTER TWO

Securities Issuances

Means a private or public offering, sale, issuance or delivery of, or commitment or agreement to commit to offer, sell, issue or deliver (whether through the issuance or granting of options, warrants, commitments, subscriptions, rights to purchase or otherwise) any stock of any class, any limited partnership interests or units, or any other debt or equity securities (including, without limitation, indebtedness having the right to vote, indebtedness convertible into any equity of any class or any other securities), or equity equivalents of either (including, without limitation, stock appreciation rights). Securities Issuance shall also mean any reorganization, recapitalization, reclassification, stock dividend, stock split, combination of shares, exchange of shares for other shares of the companies, repurchase or redemption of shares, change in corporate structure or the like in which the outstanding securities would be increased, decreased or changed into or exchanged for a different number or kind of securities.

Excluding

(1) Securities issued by a Subsidiary of the Borrower to the Borrower or to another Subsidiary and debt Securities issued by the Borrower to a Subsidiary

(2) Securities issued by the Borrower or any Subsidiary of the Borrower to shareholders in the Target for the purpose of effecting the Acquisition

(3) refinancings, refundings, renewals or extensions of Debt outstanding on the Effective Date, without increasing the principal amount thereof

(4) the issuance of notes pursuant to credit agreements with commercial banks or other financial institutions party to such credit agreements

(5) the issuance of commercial paper in the ordinary course of business

(6) the Kern River Issuance

(7) the WCG Structured Financing

(8) securities, including options, warrants or other convertible securities, issued to officers, employees, directors, consultants and certain other qualified persons pursuant to option plans or similar plans or agreements adopted by the Board of Directors of the Borrower or a Subsidiary

(9) shares of stock issued to a member of the Board of Directors of the Borrower or a Subsidiary of the Borrower for purposes of qualification

a. **Equity Financings: copies of any stock purchase agreements**

Equity financing is the process of raising capital through the sale of shares. Companies raise money because they might have a short-term need to pay bills or need funds for a long-term project that promotes growth. By selling shares, a business effectively sells ownership in its company in return for cash.

Equity financing involves the sale of common stock and the sale of other equity or quasi-equity instruments such as preferred stock, convertible preferred stock, and equity units that include common shares and warrants. A startup that grows into a successful company will have several rounds of equity financing as it evolves. Since a startup typically attracts different types of investors at various stages of its evolution, it may use different equity instruments for its financing needs. For example, angel investors and venture capitalists—generally the first investors in a startup—favor convertible preferred shares rather than common stock in exchange for funding new companies because the former have more significant upside potential and some downside protection. Once a company has grown large enough to consider going public, it may consider selling common stock to institutional and retail investors. Later, if the company needs additional capital, it may choose secondary equity financing options, such as a rights offering or an offering of equity units that includes warrants as a sweetener.

- Co-financing Agreement means the agreement to be entered into between the Recipient and the Co-financier providing for the Co-financing.
- Original Financing Agreement means the development credit agreement for a Social Investment Program Project between the Recipient and the Association.

- Collateral Acquisition Agreements means each of the agreements entered into by the Issuer in relation to the purchase by the Issuer of Collateral Debt Obligations from time to time.
- Investment Agreements or "Flow-Through Agreements" means written agreements pursuant to which the Partnership will subscribe for Flow-Through Shares (including Flow-Through Shares issued as part of a unit) or agreements by the Partnership to otherwise invest in or purchase securities of a Resource Issuer, and in respect of Flow-Through Shares comprised of units, the Resource Issuer will covenant and agree:
- Exit Facility Documents means, collectively, the Exit Facility Agreement and any related agreements, documents, and instruments delivered or entered into in connection with the Exit Facility, including any guarantee agreements, pledge and collateral agreements, intercreditor agreements, and other security documents related to or executed in connection therewith, which shall be in form and substance consistent with the RSA and the Restructuring Term Sheet.
- Credit Facility Documents means the collective reference to any Credit Facility, any notes issued pursuant thereto and the guarantees thereof, and the collateral documents relating thereto, as amended, supplemented, restated, renewed, refunded, replaced, restructured, repaid, refinanced or otherwise modified, in whole or in part, from time to time.

a. **Debt Financings: copies of convertible debt agreements**

Debt financing occurs when a firm raises money for working capital or capital expenditures by selling debt instruments to individuals and/or institutional investors. In return for lending the money, the individuals or institutions become creditors and receive a promise that the principal and interest on the debt will be repaid. The other way to raise capital in debt markets is to issue shares of stock in a public offering; this is called equity financing.

- Debt financing occurs when a company raises money by selling debt instruments to investors.
- Debt financing is the opposite of equity financing, which entails issuing stock to raise money.

- Debt financing occurs when a firm sells fixed income products, such as bonds, bills, or notes.
- Unlike equity financing where the lenders receive stock, debt financing must be paid back.
- Small and new companies, especially, rely on debt financing to buy resources that will facilitate growth.

Convertible debt definition: With convertible debt, a business borrows money from a lender or investor where both parties enter the agreement with the intent (from the outset) to repay all (or part) of the loan by converting it into a certain number of its preferred or common shares at some point in the future. The agreement specifies the repayment and conversion terms which include the timeframe and the price per share for the conversion as well as the interest rate that will be paid until either conversion or maturity. Convertible debt (also called convertible notes) is a form of financing that is often used by high-growth early-stage companies. It starts off as a loan (debt), but the lender and the company have options to convert the debt to equity under certain predetermined terms called "conversion privileges" as specified in the deal's term sheet. Under such an agreement, the lender generally does not place a valuation on the borrowing company, meaning the current or future value of the company might not be taken into account when the loan is being made. However, in many circumstances, a valuation cap (ceiling) is included in the terms. The lender may add other specific clauses to the note that they would require when and if they become a shareholder.

The agreement sometimes includes a "callable option" which allows the borrower to force conversion when the value of its shares reaches a certain threshold or a minimum financing threshold is reached while the note is outstanding (typically for two or three years). This type of financing is typically provided by a venture capital firm, angel investor or debt lender. Lenders or would be investors like convertible debt because it can provide them with interest payments for the duration of the note, discounts typically ranging from 10% to 20% on the ultimate conversion value, and priority ranking over the preferred shares or common shares as outlined in the term sheet until they decide to convert the outstanding debt into equity.

a. **Stock option or purchase plans and forms of option or purchase agreements which have been or may be used thereunder**

A stock option (also known as an equity option), gives an investor the right, but not the obligation, to buy or sell a stock at an agreed-upon price and date. There are two types of options: puts, which is a bet that a stock will fall, or calls, which is a bet that a stock will rise. Because it has shares of stock (or a stock index) as its underlying asset, stock options are a form of equity derivative and may be called equity options. Employee stock options (ESOs) are a type of equity compensation given by companies to some employees or executives that effectively amount to call options. These differ from listed equity options on stocks that trade in the market, as they are restricted to a particular corporation issuing them to their own employees.

- Stock options give a trader the right, but not the obligation, to buy or sell shares of a certain stock at an agreed-upon price and date.
- Stock options are a common form of equity derivative.
- One equity options contract generally represents 100 shares of the underlying stock.
- There are two primary types of options contract: calls and puts.
- Employee stock options (ESOs) are when a company effectively grants call options to certain employees.

Options are a type of financial instrument known as a derivative—i.e., their worth is based on, or derived from, the value of an underlying security or asset. In the case of stock options, that asset is shares of a company's stock. Essentially, the option is a contract that creates an agreement between two parties to have the option to sell or buy the stock at some point in the future at a specified price, known as the strike price (exercise price).

Stock options come in two basic forms:

Call options afford the holder the right, but not the obligation, to buy the asset at a stated price within a specific timeframe.

Put options afford the holder the right, but not the obligation, to sell the asset at a stated price within a specific timeframe.

d. **Any other agreements relating to sales of securities by the company.**

Need to cross check has company entered into any other provisional agreement to raise fund

CHAPTER THREE

Financial Matters

Financial management is one of the most important part of any business. The activities of every aspect of a business have an impact on the company's financial performance and must be evaluated and controlled by the business owner.

In its normal operations, a company provides a product or service, makes a sale to its customer, collects the money and starts the process over again. Financial management is moving cash efficiently through this cycle. This means that managing the turnover ratios of raw materials and finished goods inventories, selling to customers and collecting the receivables on a timely basis and starting over by purchasing more raw materials. In the meantime, the business must pay its bills, its suppliers and employees. All of this must be done with cash, and it takes astute financial management to make sure that these funds flow efficiently. Even though economies have a long-term history of going up, occasionally they will also experience sharp declines. Businesses must plan to have enough liquidity to weather these economic downturns, otherwise they may need to close their doors for lack of cash.

Business Operations: Every business is responsible for providing reports of its operations. Need to check other types of reports, with key performance indicators, which measure the activities of different parts of their businesses. As well, a comprehensive financial management system is able to produce the various types of reports needed by all of these different entities.

Billing strategy: Every business owner has a client that is consistently late on its invoices and payments. Managing business finances also means managing cash flow to ensure business is operating at a healthy level on a day-to-day basis. Too much cash tied up in unpaid invoices can lead to cash flow problems, a leading cause of business failure.

Debt funding: Debt funding is a loan that your company repays with added interest. Through debt financing, you can quickly access capital that you might not otherwise be able to get for weeks or even months. Bank loans, government loans, merchant cash advances, business credit lines and business credit cards are all forms of debt financing, which you must repay even if your company fails.

Equity funding: Equity funding, unlike debt funding, does not require repayment if your business fails. However, you will likely have to grant your funders a seat at the decision-making table. Venture capitalists, angel investors and equity crowd funding are all forms of equity funding.

Filing and Paying Taxes: The government is always around to collect taxes. Financial management must plan to pay its taxes on a timely basis. Financial management is an important skill of every business owner or manager. Every decision that an owner makes has a financial impact on the company, and he has to make these decisions within the total context of the company's operations.

Cash flows: Cash flow is an essential factor of business finance that ensures regular inflow of cash and the outflow of money is in the right direction. Financial management deals with all the aspects of cash flow, including credit management and taking care of outstanding payments.

Financial reporting: Every business needs to maintain its financial records, such as P&L account: cash Flow statement, balance sheet, and journals, to have a clear picture of its finances. And also to meet statutory regulations. Proper financial management enables you to keep your books up to date at all times.

Clashes with Taxation Departments: No business wants to have the Tax department at their doorstep for an audit one fine morning. The best way to avoid that is to file your taxes on time and ensure that your books are in order. A proper financial system will take care of both these aspects, and you won't have to worry about anything, even if there is an audit.

Financial Performance

Financial performance is a complete evaluation of a company's overall standing in categories such as assets, liabilities, equity, expenses, revenue, and overall profitability. It is measured through various business-related formulas that allow users to calculate exact details regarding a company's potential effectiveness. For internal users, financial performance is examined to determine their respective companies' well-being and standing, among other benchmarks. For external users, financial performance is analyzed to dictate potential investment opportunities and to determine if a company is worth their while. Before calculations can be made on certain financial indicators that establish overall performance, a financial statement analysis must occur.

Financial Statement Analysis

Financial statement analysis is a process conducted on organizations by internal and external parties to gain a better understanding of how a company is performing. The process consists of analyzing four critical financial statements in a business. The four statements that are extensively studied are a company's balance sheet, income statement, cash flow statement, and annual report.

Balance Sheet: In financial statement analysis, an organization's balance sheet is looked at to determine the operational efficiency of a business. Firstly, asset analysis is conducted and is primarily focused on more important assets such as cash and cash equivalents, inventory, and PP&E, which help predict future growth. Next, long-term and short-term liabilities are examined in order to determine if there are any future liquidity problems or debt-repayment that the organization may not be able to cover. Lastly, a company's owner's equity section is inspected, allowing the user to determine the share capital distributed inside and outside of the organization. Assets are what a company uses to operate its business. Liabilities refer to money that's borrowed from other sources and needs to be repaid by the company. Owners' equity represents the financing that owners, whether private or public, put into the business. It's important to note that assets should always be equal to the sum of liabilities and owners' equity. This relationship is the basis of the accounting equation: Assets = Liabilities + Owners' Equity

The balance sheet provides information on a company's financial health by helping you analyze the following:

- How much debt the company has relative to equity
- How liquid the business is in the short term (less than one year)
- What percentage of assets are tangible and what percentage comes from financial transactions
- How long it takes to receive outstanding payments from customers and repay suppliers
- How long it takes to sell inventory the business keeps on hand

Income Statement: In financial statement analysis, a business's income statement is investigated to determine overall present and future profitability. Examining a company's previous and current fiscal years income statement enables the user to determine if there is a trend in revenue and expenses, which in turn, shows the potential to increase future profitability.

The income statement generally starts with the revenue earned for the period minus the cost of production for goods sold to determine the gross profit. It then subtracts all other expenses, including staff salaries, rent, electricity, and non-cash expenses, such as depreciation, to determine the earnings before interest and tax (EBIT). Finally, it deducts money paid for interest and tax to determine the net profit that remains for owners. This money can be paid out as dividends or reinvested back into the company. The income statement provides information on a company's financial health by helping you analyze the following:

- How much revenue is growing over certain accounting periods
- The gross profit margin for goods sold
- What percentage of revenue results in net profit after all expenses
- If the business can cover its interest repayments on debt
- How much the business repays to shareholders versus how much it reinvests

Financial Ratio Analysis: Financial ratios help you make sense of the numbers presented in financial statements, and are powerful tools for determining the overall financial health of your company. Ratios fall under a variety of categories, including profitability, liquidity, solvency, efficiency, and valuation.

Some of the financial ratios you should know include:

- Gross profit margin: The percentage of profit the company generates after direct cost of sales expenses have been deducted from the revenue
- Net profit margin: The percentage of profit the company generates after all expenses have been deducted from revenue, including interest and tax from revenue
- Coverage ratio: The company's ability to meet its financial obligations, specifically to cover its debt and related interest payments

- Current ratio: The company's ability to meet short-term obligations of less than one year
- Quick ratio: The company's ability to meet short-term obligations of less than one year using only highly liquid assets
- Debt-to-equity ratio: The percentage of debt versus equity that the company uses to finance itself
- Inventory turnover: How many times per period the entire inventory was sold
- Total asset turnover: How efficiently the company generates revenue from total assets
- Return on equity (ROE): The company's ability to use equity investments to earn profit
- Return on assets (ROA): The company's ability to manage and use its assets to earn profit

Financial ratios should be compared across periods and against competitors to see whether your company is improving or declining, and how it's faring against direct and indirect competitors in the industry. No single ratio or statement is sufficient to analyze the overall financial health of your organization. Instead, a combination of ratio analyses across all statements should be used.

Cash Flow Statement: A cash flow statement is critical in a financial statement analysis in order to identify where the money is generated and spent by the organization. If one segment of the business is experiencing large outflows, in order to stay viable, the company must be generating inflows through financing or sales of assets.

The cash flow statement is one of the most important documents used to analyze a company's finances, as it provides key insights into the generation and use of cash. The income statement and balance sheet are based around accrual accounting, which doesn't necessarily match the actual cash movements of the business. That's why the cash flow statement exists—to remove the impacts of non-cash transactions and provide a clearer financial picture to managers, owners, and investors. The cash flow statement provides information on a company's financial health by helping you analyze the following:

- The liquidity situation of the company
- The company's sources of cash

- The free cash flow the company generates to further invest in assets or operations
- Whether overall cash has increased or decreased

Annual Report: The last statement, the annual report, provides qualitative information which is useful to further analyze a company's overall operational and financing activities. The annual report consists of all the statements listed above but adds additional insights and narratives on critical figures within the organization. The additional insights and narratives within the annual report include an extensive narrative breakdown of the various business segments, benchmarks, and overall growth. As a whole, financial performance analysis is critical whether it is conducted for internal or external use because it helps determine a business's potential future growth, structure, effectiveness, and most importantly, performance.

Measuring Financial Performance

Through a financial performance analysis, specific financial formulas and ratios are calculated, which, when compared to historical and industry metrics, provide insight into a company's financial condition and performance.

When calculating financial performance, there are seven critical ratios that are extensively used in the business world to assist and evaluate a company's overall performance.

Gross Profit Margin: The gross profit margin is a ratio that measures the remaining amount of revenue that is left after deducting the cost of sales. The ratio is useful because it indicates as a percentage the portion of each sales dollar that can be applied to cover a company's operating expenses.

Gross Profit Margin

$$\frac{(\text{Revenue} - \text{Cost of Sales})}{\text{Revenue}} \times 100$$

Enter Caption

Working Capital: The working capital measurement is used to determine an organization's liquid net assets available to fund day-to-day operations. Determining liquidity in a business is important because it indicates whether a company owns resources that can quickly be converted to cash if needed.

Working Capital

Current Assets – Current Liabilities

Enter Caption

Current Ratio: The current ratio is a liquidity ratio that helps a business determine if it owns enough current assets to cover or pay for its current liabilities.

Current Ratio

$$\frac{\text{Current Assets}}{\text{Current Liabilities}}$$

Enter Caption

Inventory Turnover Ratio: The inventory turnover ratio is an efficiency ratio that is used to measure the number of times a company sells its average inventory in a fiscal year. The ratio is beneficial because it allows the organization to easily determine if their inventory is in demand, obsolete, or if they are carrying too much.

Inventory Turnover

$$\frac{(\text{Cost of Sales})}{(\text{Beginning Inventory} + \text{Ending Inventory}) / (2)}$$

Enter Caption

Leverage: Leverage is an equity multiplier that is calculated by a business to illustrate how much debt is actually being used to buy assets. The leverage multiplier remains at one if all assets are financed by equity, but it begins to increase as more and more debt is used to purchase assets.

Leverage

$$\frac{\text{Total Assets}}{\text{Total Equity}}$$

Enter Caption

Return on Assets: Return on assets, as the name suggests, helps an organization determine how well its assets are being employed to become more profitable. If the assets are not being used effectively, the company's return on assets sum will be low.

Return on Assets

$$\frac{\text{Net Profit}}{(\text{Beginning Assets} + \text{Ending Assets}) / (2)}$$

Enter Caption

Return on Equity: Similar to return on assets, the return on equity is a profitability ratio that is used to analyze the equity effectiveness, which, in turn, earns profits for investors. A higher return on equity suggests that investors are earning at a much more efficient rate, which is more profitable to the business as a whole.

Return on Equity

$$\frac{\text{Net Profit}}{(\text{Beginning Equity} + \text{Ending Equity}) / (2)}$$

Enter Caption

Prominent financial performance metrics are as follows:

Gross Profit Margin: The ratio determines firms' profitability before considering the operating expenses. Its formula is as follows:

Gross Profit Margin = [(Revenue – Cost of Goods Sold) / Revenue] × 100.

Net Profit Margin: The net profit ratio is another financial performance metric. It measures firms' profitability after deducting all the expenses from gross profits. It is evaluated as follows:

Net Profit Margin = (Net Profit / Revenue) × 100.

Return On Equity: It is a profitability measure that ascertains a firm's ability to generate profit from equity capital that was acquired from the shareholders. It is represented by:

Return on Equity = Net Profit / [(Beginning Equity + Ending Equity) / 2].

Return On Asset: This profitability ratio determines a firm's ability to utilize assets efficiently to generate profits. Its formula is as follows:

Return On Asset = Net Profit / [(Beginning Total Assets + Ending Total Assets) / 2].

Quick Ratio: It is a liquidity metric; it analyzes firms' ability to clear short-term liabilities using cash and cash equivalents. Its formula is as follows:

Quick Ratio = (Current Assets – Inventory) / Current Liabilities.

Current Ratio: It measures firms' liquidity. It evaluates a firm's ability to pay off short-term liabilities (using current assets). It is determined as follows:

Current Ratio = Current Assets / Current Liabilities.

Working Capital: It gives an overview of a company's operational liquidity—whether a firm is efficient in handling business operations. It is evaluated as follows:

Working Capital = Current Assets – Current Liabilities.

Operating Cash Flow: Cash flow is a good indication of a firm's financial performance. This ratio analyzes a company's efficiency in maintaining a positive cash flow. This data can be acquired from companies' cash flow statements—it can be positive or negative.

Debt Asset Ratio: It is a leverage ratio; it measures a firm's ability to fulfill its short-term obligations, long-term obligations, and debts. This ratio considers companies' overall assets as the criteria. It is computed as follows:

Debt Asset Ratio = Total Debt / Total Assets.

Debt-To-Equity Ratio: It is a liquidity indicator; it is evaluated as the proportion of external liability to internal equity. It is computed as follows:

Debt-to-Equity Ratio = Total Debt / Total Equity.

Equity Multiplier: It is a proportion of assets to shareholders' equity. It indicates how much equity and debt was used to buy a particular asset. It is represented by:

Leverage = Total Assets / Total Equity.

Total Asset Turnover: It measures the maximum net sales generated by a business when it employs all its assets. It is computed as follows:

Total Asset Turnover = Net Sales / Total Sales.

Inventory Turnover: This ratio measures companies' ability to convert stock into sales:

Inventory Turnover = Cost of Inventory Sold / Average Inventory.

Accounts Receivable Turnover: It gauges firms' efficiency in recovering outstanding credit (sales) from the debtors. It is evaluated as follows:

Accounts Receivable Turnover = Net Credit Sales / Average Accounts Receivables.

Accounts Payable Turnover: This indicator evaluates a company's ability to repay creditors (goods purchased on credit). It is calculated as follows:

Accounts Payable Turnover = Net Credit Purchase / Average Accounts Payable.

Checklist of Financial Statement Checklist

- Company's annual, quarterly, and (if available) monthly financial statements for the last three years reveal about its financial performance and condition?
- Audited company's financial statements
- All liabilities of the company, both current and contingent
- Margins for the business growing or deteriorating
- Company's projections for the future and underlying assumptions
- Company's projections for the current year
- What normalized working capital will be necessary to continue running the business
- How is "working capital" determined for purposes of the acquisition agreement? (Definitional differences can result in a large variance of the dollar number.)
- Capital expenditures and other investments will need to be made to continue growing the business, and what are the company's current capital commitments?
- The condition of assets
- Indebtedness outstanding or guaranteed by the company, what are its terms, and when does it have to be repaid.
- Any unusual revenue recognition issues for the company or the industry in which it operates
- The aging of accounts receivable, and are there any other accounts receivable issues
- Quality of earnings" report be commissioned

- Capital and operating budgets appropriate, or have necessary capital expenditures been deferred
- EBITDA and any adjustments to EBITDA been appropriately calculated (This is particularly important if the buyer is obtaining debt financing.)
- Company have sufficient financial resources to both continue operating in the ordinary course and cover its transaction expenses between the time of diligence and the anticipated closing date of the acquisition

CHAPTER FOUR

Licenses and Permits

Business licenses are required by the government in order to increase accountability, transparency, and consumer protection. These organizations may be difficult to deal with if you don't have the appropriate business licenses, and they sometimes have the power to impose fines or even close down non – compliance businesses. A home-based or internet firm may also need to seek business licenses, so be aware that they aren't simply necessary for enterprises with actual locations. Even though it might be time-consuming, getting all the required company permits up front can reduce stress and costs in the long run.

There are different forms of companies as per the Companies Act, 2013:

One Person Company (OPC): One Person Company registration was introduced in 2013 and enables a sole proprietor to form their company and conduct lawful commercial operations.

Private Limited Company (PLC):This type of business tries to limit its owners to particular social classes. A Public Limited Company (PLC) differs from a private limited company in several ways.

Public Limited Company: A Public Limited Company differs from a Private Limited Company in that it is able to invite the entire public to become shareholders without expressing any preference for any particular group.

Sole Proprietorship Company (SPC): A Sole Proprietorship firm is a business entity that is owned, controlled and managed by a single person. The owner of the business is called the sole proprietor of the firm. The promoter himself receives all the profits.

Partnership Firm: Partners who have agreed on the role and profit sharing are the ones who manage operations in partnerships. The partnership agreement is a verbal agreement that specifies the roles, responsibilities, authority, and number of shares owned.

Types of Business Licenses in India

The Ministry of Corporate Affairs oversees the registration of companies and Limited Liability Partnerships (LLPs) in India. A company's registration grants it a continuous existence, a separate legal identity, and limited liability protection. Registration will assist the firm in growing and expanding gradually after turnover surpasses a particular threshold.

GST Registration: Businesses with intrastate supply and business entities with turnover above the set threshold limit must register under the Goods and Services Tax. Businesses must compulsorily register under GST in order to meet a number of extra requirements. For new firms, GST registration must be completed online within a certain time frame. Find a list of the necessary paperwork to register a business for GST.

Udyam Aadhar Registration: The Udyam online site handles India's small businesses. Although Udyam Aadhar registration is not required, there are several advantages to registering, including government credit programmes, subsidies, etc. The requirements for Udyam registration are specified in terms of a composite criteria that takes into account business revenue and investment in machinery and plants.

FSSAI Registration or License (In case you wish to start a business of edibles): This is the national authority for ensuring the safety and standardization of food items in India. FSSAI stands for Food Safety and Standard Authority of India. All retail establishments, trade outlets, kiosks, eateries, caterers, and cloud kitchens must follow to FSSAI regulations, get licenses, and periodically renew their registrations. The following categories apply to the license or registration requirement:

FSSAI Basic Registration: Up to Rs. 12 lakh in revenue.

FSSAI State License: For revenue between Rs 12 lakh and Rs 20 crore.

FSSAI Central License: For Revenue above Rs. 20 billion.

Import Export Code (For businesses doing import and export of goods and services): In India, export and import companies are required to have a unique license known as the Import Export Code, which is issued by the Directorate General of Foreign Trade under the Ministry of Commerce. Registration can be achieved online by submitting the legally essential papers on the DGFT website. A PAN card, an identification card with address verification, evidence of business residency, proof of a current bank account, etc. are required in documentation.

Opening a Retail Store in India Requires a License: Under the "Shop and Establishments Act," a license is required to operate a retail store in India. Since State Governments are in charge of issuing registrations, the rules in India vary from one state to the next. The Act governs all local stores and businesses and keeps an eye on how they behave to ensure that there is no child labor, excessive working hours, unhealthy circumstances, unfair wage practices, etc.

Trade License: Many small company owners are turning to the internet as their preferred method of conducting business because there are so many simple online business loans accessible for MSMEs. A sole proprietorship is the most practical form of company for small companies since there are fewer regulations to follow. Under the Shop and Establishments Act, a sole proprietorship can apply for a trade license in the same way as a conventional shop.

Licenses needed for an Indian Factory: Under the Factories Act of 1948, registration is required to operate a factory in India which is granted by the state government. According to the type of company and state laws governing safety, welfare, and labor standards, there can be extra permission requirements.

Additional Licensing and Registration: There are many more company categories that are not included in the list above. Wherever it is judged essential, the government requires licenses and permits to guarantee the welfare of the public and the environment. For example, the Insurance Regulatory and Development Authority supervises insurance firms, while the Reserve Bank of India oversees the banking and microfinance industries.

Checklist

a. Copies of any governmental licenses, permits or consents.
b. Any correspondence or documents relating to any proceedings of any regulatory agency.

CHAPTER FIVE

Shareholder Information

Types of Shareholders: Many companies issue two types of stock: common and preferred. Common stock is more prevalent than preferred stock, and is what ordinary investors typically buy in the stock market. Generally, common stockholders enjoy voting rights, but preferred stockholders do not. However, preferred stockholders have a priority claim to dividends. Furthermore, the dividends paid to preferred stockholders are generally more significant than those paid to common stockholders.

A majority shareholder owns and controls more than 50% of a company's outstanding shares. This type of shareholder is often company founders or their descendants. Minority shareholders hold less than 50% of a company's stock, even as little as one share.

Some key shareholder rights: Shareholders have the right to inspect the company's books and records, the power to sue the corporation for the misdeeds of its directors and/or officers, and the right to vote on critical corporate matters, such as naming board directors. In addition, they have the right to decide whether or not to green-light potential mergers, the right to receive dividends, the right to attend annual meetings, the right to vote on crucial matters by proxy, and the right to claim a proportionate allocation of proceeds if a company liquidates its assets.

The difference between preferred and common shareholders: The main difference between preferred and common shareholders is that the former typically has no voting rights, while the latter does. However, preferred shareholders have a priority claim to income, meaning that they are paid dividends before common shareholders. Common shareholders are last in line regarding company assets, which means that they will be paid out after creditors, bondholders, and preferred shareholders.

Checklist:

a. Records setting forth all issuances or grants of stock, options, and warrants by the Company, listing the names of the issues or grantees, the amounts issued or granted, the dates of the issuances or grants, the number of shares presently exercisable, and the consideration received (or to be received) by the company in each case
b. Lists of all current shareholders
c. Numerical listing of stock certificates showing certificate number and date, name of shareholder, number of shares, date of board approval, and permit and tracing transfers
d. Lists of all options proposed to be granted

CHAPTER SIX

Material Contracts

Means any contract or other arrangement (other than Loan Documents), whether written or oral, to which any Credit Party is a party as to which the breach, nonperformance, cancellation or failure to renew by any party thereto could reasonably be expected to have a Material Adverse Effect

a. **Bank line of credit agreements**

As an arrangement between a financial institution—usually a bank—and a customer that establishes the maximum loan amount that the customer can borrow. The borrower can access funds from the LOC at any time as long as they do not exceed the maximum amount (or credit limit) set in the agreement. With respect to the Issuer or any of its Subsidiaries, one or more debt facilities, indentures or other arrangements (including the Credit Agreement or commercial paper facilities and overdraft facilities) with banks, other financial institutions or investors providing for revolving credit loans, term loans, notes, receivables financing (including through the sale of receivables to such institutions or to special purpose entities formed to borrow from such institutions against such receivables), letters of credit or other Indebtedness, in each case, as amended, restated, modified, renewed, refunded, replaced, restructured, refinanced, repaid, increased or extended in whole or in part from time to time (and whether in whole or in part and whether or not with the original administrative agent and lenders or another administrative agent or agents or other banks or institutions and whether provided under the original Credit Agreement or one or more other credit or other agreements, indentures, financing agreements or otherwise) and in each case including all agreements, instruments and documents executed and delivered pursuant to or in connection with the foregoing (including any notes and letters of credit issued pursuant thereto and any Guarantee and collateral agreement, patent and trademark security agreement, mortgages or letter of credit applications and other Guarantees, pledges, agreements, security agreements and collateral documents). Without limiting the generality of the foregoing, the term "Credit Facility" shall include any agreement or instrument (1) changing the maturity of any Indebtedness Incurred thereunder or contemplated thereby, (2) adding Subsidiaries of the Issuer as additional borrowers or guarantors thereunder, (3) increasing the amount of Indebtedness Incurred thereunder or available to be borrowed thereunder or (4) otherwise altering the terms and conditions thereof.

Demand -Term loans- Demand loans repayable in predetermined installments. If repayment exceeds 36 months, it is term loan.

CC- Granted against security of stock, book debts without any stipulation of repayment but to be renewed every year. If borrower draws beyond Sanction-limit/ Drawing power, it is Temporary Over-limit

OD- Similar to CC but can be unsecured or security is other than stock or book debts (eg- FD receipts, NSC, LIC policies, shares etc.)

Bills purchased/Discounted An advance against a sale bill granted to a seller with condition that it is repaid before physical possession of goods passes to a buyer Bills purchase. An advance granted against a sale bill, wherein a buyer has received goods & has agreed to pay amounts within a stipulated period - Bills discounted.

Statements to be obtained

- Accounting policies & Closing Guidelines
- Statements generated on 31st March:

Facility - Party wise list of accounts outstanding with overdue over Sanctioned limit / DP Sanctioning powers of branch officials & higher authorities

List of accounts where ad hoc or regular facility is due for renewal but not renewed - where stock and book debts statements are in arrears – inadequate insurance – overdue stock audits - For CC and OD A/cs month wise debit and credit transactions (turnover)

NPA statements

Checklist :

Loan Documents. The following documents for the Loan: (1) the Note; (2) Security Agreements granting to Lender security interests in the Collateral; (3) financing statements and all other documents perfecting Lender's Security Interests; (4) evidence of insurance as required below;

(5) guaranties; (6) together with all such Related Documents as Lender may require for the Loan; all in form and substance satisfactory to Lender and Lender's counsel.

Borrower's Authorization. Borrower must have provided in form and substance satisfactory to Lender properly certified resolutions, duly authorizing the execution and delivery of this Agreement, the Note and the Related Documents. In addition, Borrower must have provided such other resolutions, authorizations, documents and instruments as Lender or its counsel, may require.

Fees and Expenses under This Agreement. Borrower must have paid to Lender all fees, costs, and expenses specified in this Agreement and the Related Documents as are then due and payable.

Representations and Warranties. The representations and warranties set forth in this Agreement, in the Related Documents, and in any document or certificate delivered to Lender under this Agreement are true and correct.

No Event of Default. There shall not exist at the time of any Advance a condition which would constitute an Event of Default under this Agreement or under any Related Document.

Litigation and Claims. No litigation, claim, investigation, administrative proceeding or similar action (including those for unpaid taxes) against Borrower is pending or threatened, and no other event has occurred which may materially adversely affect Borrower's financial condition or properties, other than litigation, claims, or other events, if any, that have been disclosed to and acknowledged by Lender in writing.

Taxes. To the best of Borrower's knowledge, all of Borrower's tax returns and reports that are or were required to be filed, have been filed, and all taxes, assessments and other governmental charges have been paid in full, except those presently being or to be contested by Borrower in good faith in the ordinary course of business and for which adequate reserves have been provided.

Lien Priority. Unless otherwise previously disclosed to Lender in writing, Borrower has not entered into or granted any Security Agreements, or permitted the filing or attachment of any Security Interests on or affecting any of the Collateral directly or indirectly securing repayment of Borrower's Loan and Note, that would be prior or that may in any way be superior to Lender's Security Interests and rights in and to such Collateral.

Binding Effect. This Agreement, the Note, all Security Agreements (if any), and all Related Documents are binding upon the signers thereof, as well as upon their successors, representatives and assigns, and are legally enforceable in accordance with their respective terms.

False Statements. Any warranty, representation or statement made or furnished to Lender by Borrower or on Borrower's behalf under this Agreement or the Related Documents is false or misleading in any material respect, either now or at the time made or furnished or becomes false or misleading at any time thereafter.

a. **Other agreements evidencing outstanding loans to or guarantees by the company**

During audit need to check are there any outstanding loans (Banks, private landers etc) also need to check against which guarantee they have taken loan

c. **All outstanding leases for real and personal property**

Need to cross check all lease agreements and payout to avoid outstanding loan disputes in future

d. **Material contracts with suppliers or customers, indicating which suppliers are sole source**

A sole source is defined as the only supplier that can provide you with the goods or products you need. The sole source has either established a monopoly or is the only provider within a geographic region from which business owners can obtain what they need. In some instances, the sole source is the choice because it is the only vendor available at a specific time that can handle what a business owner requires, or it is the only vendor that carries that product. For example, a vendor who carries automobile parts that are no longer manufactured is considered a sole source because any company that needs that part must sign a contract with that specific vendor.

Sole Source Justification Criteria

A Sole Source justification describes the steps taken to determine that the chosen supplier is the only source available for your product/service. The following list of criteria may be used in determining if a sole source situation exists:

1. Only one manufacturer makes the item meeting required specifications; that manufacturer only sells direct or exclusively through one regional/ national distributor; Describe the steps taken to determine only one source exists.
2. Item must be identical to equipment already in use to ensure compatibility with existing equipment or systems, and that item is only available from one source. Provide a previous po number or equipment inventory tag number in your sole source justification.
3. Named in award: Supplier is specifically named by the funding source award documents, inter-agency agreement, or clinical trials agreement. Proposal documents are not considered an "award document".
4. Maintenance or repair by the original equipment manufacturer (OEM) and the manufacturer does not have multiple agents to perform these services.
5. Replacement or spare parts are required from the OEM, and the OEM does not have distributors for those parts.
6. Patented items or copyrighted materials, which are only available from the patent or copyright holder.
7. A medical/surgical decision by a medical/dental professional, where a specific brand is required for patient care, and the manufacturer has no distributors for the product.
8. Consultants only: The chosen Consultant has unique expertise, background in recognized field of endeavor, the result of which may depend primarily on the individual's invention, imagination, or talent. Consultant has advanced or specialized knowledge, or expertise gained over an extensive period of time in a specialized field of experience.
9. A Market Survey has been conducted to determine whether other suppliers capable of satisfying the requirements exist. A list of all the suppliers contacted, along with the reason why each supplier could not meet the requirements should be provided with the sole source justification.

Federally funded sole source purchases are limited to the following categories:

- the item is available only from a single source - describe the steps taken to determine there are no other suppliers
- the public exigency or emergency for the requirement will not permit a delay resulting from competitive solicitation
- the federal awarding agency or pass-through entity expressly authorizes noncompetitive proposals in response to a written request from the non-federal entity
- after solicitation of a number of sources, competition is determined inadequate

e. **Model sales or manufacturing contracts**

Types of Pricing Models: The majority of all contract manufacturing agreements encompass one or a mixture of 4 pricing models. Depending on what type of product the OEM offers, some models will be more suitable than others.

Below is an outline of how each pricing model is structured and what the key financial measurement is for the contract manufacturer.

Fixed Materials Pricing: Perhaps the simplest pricing model, fixed materials pricing locks in the material cost of goods sold (MCOGs) as a percentage of the OEM's product program revenue. It requires very little overhead to manage due to the fact that the EMS provider does not have to provide a new quote with each build program. This model is ideal for OEMs with similar types of product lines and manufacturing volumes.

Component Cost Pricing: In this model, the EMS provider determines the internal percentage costs across a number of categories such as materials, overhead and direct labour to calculate the profit it needs to cover costs. The provider can then work to improve margins internally to gain a bigger profit. Though this model is commonly used today, OEM customers can find it to be frustrating as the true costs associated with the program can remain hidden. Component cost pricing is suitable for OEMs with a mix of consumer products offering mid- to high-level technology.

Cost Plus Pricing: Often viewed as the fairest and most honest model, cost plus pricing involves the provider educating the OEM on all costs involved in running the proposed programs. Both partners agree on a fixed percentage of profit for the provider, and work together to identify new opportunities to reduce costs. The open and transparent nature of this model cultivates a healthy vendor-customer relationship where both parties are collaborating for the same goal. Cost plus pricing can be applied to most product programs across various industries and technologies.

Return on Invested Capital (ROIC): This model revolves around an ROIC formula as it relates to the EMS provider's net profits. While more complex to calculate regularly, it is the most dynamic model out of the four and nicely sets up both partners to work together for mutual benefit. Being able to change the individual component values creates a flexible system for both the provider and the customer without impacting the target ROIC, as long as the overall give and take of the equation is considered. For example, the OEM customer may request that the payments be pushed to a later date in exchange for a larger profit margin. Remember, choosing the right pricing model for your contract manufacturing agreement is only part of the work. Your goal should be focused on setting up your vendor-client relationship for long-term, mutual gain.

f. **Agreements for loans to and any other agreements with officers, directors, or employees**

Need to explore all possible angles to avoid post acquisition issues

g. **Schedule of all insurance policies in force covering property of the company and any other insurance policies such as "key person" policies, director indemnification policies, or product liability policies**

Types of insurance to consider, depending on your business: (Please note: this is only a fraction of the types of insurance available.)

Lease-Hold Insurance (covers the difference between your old and new rent amounts if you lose your old building/office. Covers the unexpired portion of a long-term lease.)

Accounts Receivable Insurance (covers your accounts receivable should you lose all of your receivables records and are hence unable to collect)

Valuable Papers Insurance (covers the coast to replace crucial documents that you lose and do not have duplicates of. Includes property titles, deeds, etc.)

Boiler & Machinery Insurance (covers damage from some event that impacts your building' s boiler and/or electrical apparatus. Often overlooked because business owners don' t realize these things aren' t covered by property insurance.)

Convention Cancellation Insurance (covers the loss of revenue resulting from the cancellation of conventions, seminars, conferences, etc. Best for companies who derive a significant amount of their annual revenues from such events.)

Key Man Insurance (essentially a life insurance policy for a person or persons whose death would result in severe financial difficulty for the company. Payment in the case of death goes to the company itself.)

Public Liability: Protects against claims of damages from third party personal injury or property damage that occurs as a result of your business related activities, either at the workplace or at another location. Includes Product Liability.

Professional Indemnity: Protects against financial losses for any legal action taken against you or your business for negligent acts, errors or omissions made in the provision of professional services or advice that you provide

Management Liability: Protects businesses and business directors, including their personal assets, against legal costs for allegations of mismanagement, misconduct or legislative breaches

Cyber Liability: Protection against the expenses and legal costs associated with data breaches, which may occur after being hacked or from theft of client information.

Contents: Covers your contents and stock against material damage loss as a result of specified events, such as fire, storm, malicious damage and other perils. Can also include benefits such as additional increases in stock during seasonal periods.

Building :Covers the cost of repairing or reconstructing your business premises (that you own) as a result of fire, storm and other perils specified in the policy.

Theft: Cover for loss or damage to contents or stock through theft or attempted theft at your premises following forced and violent entry.

General Property: Covers loss or damage to portable & valuable items, up to a specified limit, that you carry around with you during the course of your business (within country),such as tools of trade, mobile phones and laptops.

Glass Provides: cover for the costs of replacing internal or external glass that is accidentally damaged or broken, including windows, mirrors or porcelain.

Electronic Equipment: Covers your insured computers or other insured electronic equipment against loss, damage or breakdown caused by an event defined under your policy.

Machinery Breakdown: Covers the cost of repairing or replacing insured machinery following breakdown. Includes electronic or mechanical machinery and equipment, such as boilers, pressure plants, refrigerators and air conditioners.

Money: Covers money belonging to your business that is lost, stolen or damaged whilst on your premises, in transit to or from your premises, or in your personal custody.

Transit: For goods (or goods you are responsible for) whilst in transit in a vehicle owned by or operated by your business, against loss, theft or damage due to an accident or fire.

Employee Dishonesty: Covers your business against financial loss incurred through fraudulent or dishonest acts by employees. Includes cover for money, inventory and equipment.

Employment Practices: Liability Provides protection from the financial cost of employment related claims made by your employees, including allegations of unfair dismissal, defamation, bullying and harassment, discrimination, and sexual harassment. *Cover can be taken out as an option under a Business Insurance pack as an alternative to a Management Liability policy

Statutory Liability: Covers the costs and expenses incurred by official investigations or inquiries against your business as a result of innocent breaches of various Acts of Parliament, such as occupational health & safety laws and environmental laws. Includes the cost of fines and penalties. *Cover can be taken out as an option under a Business Insurance pack as an alternative to a Management Liability policy.

Personal Accident: Essential protection for you and your family against the financial costs as the result of you suffering an accident or defined illness by covering up to 85% of your income if you are temporarily unable to work. Includes the option of, either you or your beneficiaries, receiving a lump sum payment in the event of permanent disablement or death.

h. **Partnership or joint venture agreements**

When two or more individuals come together and enter into a contract to form an association to carry on a business as co-owners for the profit of the co-owners it is called Partnership. It is governed by the "Indian Partnership Act, 1932". Whereas, when two or more business entities or individuals working separately come together for specific business purposes for a limited period it is called Joint Venture (JV). They pull their resources together to achieve mutual goals. It is highly flexible which could involve either an expansion to an existing business or an entirely new business. Joint Ventures has initially been used for trading and commercial purposes by the merchants and businessmen.

Partnership agreement: When two or more individuals want to enter into a partnership, they are required to enter into a partnership agreement. The agreement states details about the business, the relationship between the partners, percentage of ownership, profit and loss percentage, etc. The agreement between the partners can be oral or written at the will of the partners. But it is always advisable to have a written agreement to avoid future disputes. Section 5 of the Partnership act states that for a partnership, the existence of an agreement is essential. It is very important to have a good agreement in place to avoid unnecessary litigation proceedings. A good partnership agreement will have solutions to all major issues that can take place in the future.

Joint venture agreement: Joint ventures have characteristics of a partnership. It can be formed between partnerships, corporations, LLP, etc. It can be formed by a larger and a smaller entity to work together on projects. It is a collaboration between two companies lacking in some aspect to use the resources of other companies without any disbursement. A joint venture agreement like the partnership agreement is formed to avoid all legal issues and to describe the roles and responsibilities of the entities coming together for business purposes.

Purpose of partnership agreement

The main objective of a partnership is to form a new business that will aid profit to its partners. The following are the main purposes for which it is recommended to have a written partnership agreement:

- Control over ownership

A Partnership agreement includes a clause relating to allotment of shares and imposes a reasonable restriction on transfer of ownership by way of transfer of shares in a company. Through a written agreement parties have a clear idea on the pattern of transfer of ownership in the event of the death of a partner. It safeguards the company to be sold to a competitor by imposing reasonable restrictions on the transfer of shares. It avoids the event of uncertainty. In many cases, it protects the shareholding percentage of an existing partner in the event of a change in the share capital of the company.

- Avoid legal issue

In the event when properly written provisions are not made, it can invite unnecessary legal suits on the point of disagreement between partners. These agreements are made by foreseeing possible events of disagreement and by inserting clauses to avoid the same. This can protect partners from costly legal issues. For instance, after the business starts making profit there are mainly two questions raised. First, when can the partners take money out of business and second, how much will each partner get. In case when there is no written agreement providing answers to these questions, it can amount to legal issues between the partners.

- Describe roles and responsibilities

Partnership agreements provide the roles of each partner towards the business of the Partnership. It lays responsibilities on partners to provide true accounts of the business. It states the provision of compensation to partners due to loss incurred by the fraudulent act of the other partner or partners.

- Avoid tax issues

A partnership firm is not termed as a separate legal entity. Therefore, there is a tax liability imposed on individual partners. It means every partner is liable to pay tax on his share of income from the business. A written agreement about the distribution of profits and losses spells the tax status of the partnership, which helps avoid any tax issues.

Avoid the state's default rules: If there is no written partnership agreement in place then the business and the partners will be governed as per the default rules of the state. The written agreement helps partners to set their own rules and regulations as per their interest and the interest of the business.

Protect business and investments: Events like bankruptcy, partner's death, or disability can hurt the business of the firm. When there is no written agreement giving remedy during such situations, the company may go into dissolution risking the investments made by the partners. In an event when one of the partners dies, his amount of share into the Partnership can be paid to his legal representatives and other partners can continue with the business. Also, provisions are inserted that prevent the company's confidential information from being shared by partners which protects the interests of other partners and the business.

Purpose of joint venture agreement

The advantages of forming a joint venture are sharing of risk, access to larger markets, the larger capacity to produce goods and render services, etc. Therefore, to achieve these advantages successfully it is essential to have a well-structured, well-drafted, clear, and planned agreement in place. The main purposes of a written joint venture agreement are:

To list out contributions: In joint ventures, the partners come together and contribute resources like funds, goods, technological resources, etc. The agreement states the list of contributions made by the ventures. The contribution can be made either equally or more by one venture than the other.

Termination: As a joint venture is prepared for a limited number of periods, the agreement provides a termination clause defining the period after which the Joint venture will be dissolved. The agreement defines the period or the condition after which the venture will come to an end.

Responsibilities: In a joint venture, the responsibilities and obligations of the partners are limited to their part as put forth in the agreement. The agreement defines the responsibility of partners to avoid any dispute or confusion on the same.

Tax consideration: The pattern in which the joint venture will be taxed depends on its structure. The agreement defines the structure of the joint venture whether an LLP or company, etc.

Types of partnership agreement

There are different types of partnerships formed based on Objectives, Tenure, Nature, and Liability. For example, in some partnerships the objective of the partners will be to continue the partnership for a specific period while in other cases the partnership is in existence till achievement of a particular objective. In some cases all the partners may have unlimited liabilities. Whereas, in others one of the partners may have limited liability while the rest won't. Some of the types of such partnerships are:

Partnership at will: Such a partnership can be brought to an end at the will of the Partners by way of notice of mentioning his intention to do so. Its tenure solely depends on the will of the partner. Even if one of the partners sends the notice of termination the entire partnership comes to an end.

Particular partnership: This type of partnership is formed for undertaking a particular business. It comes to an end on the completion of the objective of the business. The limited period of this type of partnership depends on the condition precedent upon the happening of which the dissolution takes place.

General partnership: In the absence of a partnership agreement, the partnership is governed as per the default provisions of the Indian Partnership Act 1932. In this type the liability of each partner is unlimited.

Limited liability partnership: In this type of partnership agreement, some or all partners have limited liabilities. Partners enjoy limited personal liability only for their share of investment in the partnership. They cannot participate in the general management and daily operations of the firm.

Different types of joint venture agreement

There are different types of joint ventures. Some of the common types are:

Contractual joint venture: Contractual joint ventures is a type of Joint Venture where two or more parties come together only for specific business purposes without creating a separate legal entity. Franchisee is an example Contractual JV.

Equity joint venture: Equity means Ownership. In this type of JV a separate legal entity is created unlike Contractual JV. The partners share ownership, management, responsibilities, and profits and losses of the company. For instance, when a foreign company providing technology and other knowledge-based inputs wants to ensure managing power in the JV, this type of JV is entered into between the parties. The foreign company will have an option to invest in the JV at a future date.

Partnership joint venture: A partnership or limited liability partnership venture can be set to merge the two businesses. An example of it is one party involved in the production of goods approaching another party to use their marketing and promotion skills for selling the products.

Vertical joint venture: Vertical joint ventures are incredibly useful for dealing with importing products. This allows businesses to enter new markets while sharing risk. Both companies can work towards finding more effective ways to reach their goals by sharing industry knowledge, funding, etc.

i. Bonus plans, retirement plans, pension plans, deferred compensation plans, profit sharing, and management incentive agreements

Employee benefits are all forms of consideration given by an entity in exchange for service rendered by employees or for the termination of employment.

Short-term employee benefits are employee benefits (other than termination benefits) that are expected to be settled wholly before twelve months after the end of the annual reporting period in which the employees render the related service.

Post-employment benefits are employee benefits (other than termination benefits and short-term employee benefits) that are payable after the completion of employment.

Other long-term employee benefits are all employee benefits other than short-term employee benefits, post-employment benefits and termination benefits.

Termination benefits are employee benefits provided in exchange for the termination of an employee's employment as a result of either:

(a) an entity's decision to terminate an employee's employment before the normal retirement date; or

(b) an employee's decision to accept an offer of benefits in exchange for the termination of employment.

Service cost comprises:

(a) current service cost, which is the increase in the present value of the defined benefit obligation resulting from employee service in the current period;

(b) past service cost, which is the change in the present value of the defined benefit obligation for employee service in prior periods, resulting from a plan amendment (the introduction or withdrawal of, or changes to, a defined benefit plan) or a curtailment (a significant reduction by the entity in the number of employees covered by a plan); and

(c) any gain or loss on settlement.

Net interest on the net defined benefit liability (asset) is the change during the period in the net defined benefit liability (asset) that arises from the passage of time.

Potential Downsides

- A deferred compensation plan involves some risk. The most significant downsides are:
- Losing funds if the company goes insolvent or files bankruptcy
- Unless deferred compensation funds are in a trust, creditors can take employee accounts to settle company debts
- Creditors can even take money from employees in the event they leave a company before the company files bankruptcy (if the employee knew the company was close to bankruptcy)
- Penalties and taxes for accessing funds early
- Taking a lump sum distribution could trigger a large tax bill and penalties on the total distribution
- If an employee switches jobs or quits, they could lose their entire account
- No rollover options
- Deferred compensation plans can both increase and decrease in value, so they require careful management

j. **Form of employee confidentiality invention assignment agreement**

"Confidential Information" means trade secrets, proprietary information and materials, and confidential knowledge and information which includes, but is not limited to, matters of a technical nature (such as discoveries, ideas, concepts, designs, drawings, specifications, techniques, models, diagrams, test data, scientific methods and know-how, and materials such as reagents, substances, chemical compounds, subcellular constituents, cell or cell lines, organisms and progeny, and mutants, derivatives or replications derived from or relating to any of the foregoing materials), and matters of a business nature (such as the identity of customers and prospective customers, the nature of work being done for or discussed with customers or prospective customers, suppliers, marketing techniques and materials, marketing and development plans, pricing or pricing policies, financial information, plans for further development, and any other information of a similar nature not available to the public).

"Confidential Information" shall not include information that: (a) was in Employee's possession or in the public domain before receipt from the Company, as evidenced by the then existing publication or other public dissemination of such information in written or other documentary form; (b) becomes available to the public through no fault of Employee; (c) is received in good faith by Employee from a third party who is not subject to an obligation of confidentiality to the Company or any other party; or (d) is required by a judicial or administrative authority or court having competent jurisdiction to be disclosed by Employee, provided that Employee shall promptly notify the Company and allow the Company a reasonable time to oppose or limit such order.

NON-DISCLOSURE OF CONFIDENTIAL INFORMATION OF INSPIRE: Employee acknowledges that, during the period of Employee's employment with Inspire, Employee has had or will have access to Confidential Information of Inspire. Therefore, Employee agrees that both during and after the period of Employee's employment with Inspire, Employee shall not, without the prior written approval of Inspire, directly or indirectly (a) reveal, report, publish, disclose or transfer any Confidential Information of Inspire to any person or entity, or (b) use any Confidential Information of Inspire for any purpose or for the benefit of any person or entity, except as may be necessary in the performance of Employee's work for Inspire.

NON-DISCLOSURE OF CONFIDENTIAL INFORMATION OF OTHERS: Employee acknowledges that, during the period of Employee's employment with Inspire, Employee may have had or will have access to Confidential Information of third parties who have given Inspire the right to use such Confidential Information, subject to a non-disclosure agreement between Inspire and such third party. Therefore, Employee agrees that both during and after the period of Employee's employment with Inspire, Employee shall not, without the prior written approval of Inspire, directly or indirectly (a) reveal, report, publish, disclose or transfer any Confidential Information of such third parties to any person or entity, or (b) use any Confidential Information of such third parties for any purpose or for the benefit of any person or entity, except as may be necessary in the performance of Employee's work for Inspire.

PROPERTY OF INSPIRE: Employee acknowledges and agrees that all Confidential Information of Inspire and all reports, drawings, blueprints, materials, data, code, notes and other documents and records, whether printed, typed, handwritten, videotaped, transmitted or transcribed on data files or on any other type of media, and whether or not labeled or identified as confidential or proprietary, made or compiled by Employee, or made available to Employee, during the period of Employee employment with

Inspire (including the period prior to the date of this Agreement) concerning Inspire's Confidential Information are and shall remain Inspire's property and shall be delivered to Inspire within five (5) business days after the termination of such employment with Inspire or at any earlier time on request of Inspire. Employee shall not retain copies of such Confidential Information, documents and records.

Confidential Information.

Company Information: I agree at all times during the term of my employment and after termination, to hold in the strictest confidence, and not to use, except for the benefit of the Company Group, or to disclose to any person, corporation or other entity without written consent of the Company, any Confidential Information. I understand that "Confidential Information" means any proprietary or confidential information of the Company Group, its affiliates, their clients, customers or their partners, and the Company Group's licensors, including, without limitation, technical data, trade secrets, research and development information, product plans, services, customer lists and customers (including, but not limited to, customers of the Company Group on whom I called or with whom I became acquainted during the term of my employment), supplier lists and suppliers, software, developments, inventions, processes, formulas, technology, designs, drawings, engineering, hardware configuration information, personnel information, marketing, finances or other business information disclosed to me by or obtained by me from the Company Group, its affiliates, their clients, customers or their partners, and the Company Group's licensors either directly or indirectly in writing, orally or by drawings or observation of parts or equipment.

Company Property: I understand that all documents (including computer records, facsimile and e-mail) and materials created, received or transmitted in connection with my work or using the facilities of the Company Group are property of the Company Group and subject to inspection by the Company Group, at any time. Upon termination of my employment with the Company (or at any other time when requested by the Company), I will promptly deliver to the Company all documents and materials of any nature pertaining to my work with the Company and will provide written certification of my compliance with this Agreement. Under no circumstances will I have, following my termination, in my possession any property of the Company Group, or any documents or materials or copies thereof containing any Confidential Information. In the event of the termination of my employment, I agree to sign and deliver the Termination Certification.

Former Employer Information: I agree that I will not, during my work with the Company, improperly use or disclose any trade secrets of any other person or entity or proprietary information of any former employer or other person or entity with which I have an agreement or duty to keep in confidence such information and that I will not bring onto the premises of the Company Group any unpublished document or proprietary information belonging to any such employer, person or entity unless consented to in writing by such employer, person or entity. I agree to indemnify the Company Group and hold it harmless from all claims, liabilities, damages and expenses, including reasonable attorneys fees and costs for resolving disputes, arising out of or in connection with any violation or claimed violation of a third party's rights resulting from any use by the Company Group of such proprietary information or trade secrets improperly used or disclosed by me.

Third Party Information: I recognize that the Company Group has received and in the future will receive from third parties their confidential or proprietary information subject to a duty on the Company Group's part to maintain the confidentiality of such information and to use it only for certain limited purposes. I agree to hold all such confidential or proprietary information in the strictest confidence and not to disclose it to any person, firm or corporation or to use it except as necessary in carrying out my work for the Company consistent with the Company Group's agreement with such third party.

General Provisions.

Terms and Conditions of Employment. I acknowledge that the terms and conditions of my employment with the Company are provided for in a separate employment agreement between me and the Company and no provision of this Agreement shall be construed as conferring upon me a right to be an employee of the Company.

Governing Law. This Agreement will be governed by the laws.

Entire Agreement. This Agreement sets forth the entire agreement and understanding between the Company and me relating to the subject matter herein and merges all prior discussions between us. No modification of or amendment to this Agreement, nor any waiver of any rights under this Agreement, will be effective unless in writing signed by the party to be charged. Any subsequent change or changes in my duties, salary or compensation will not affect the validity or scope of this Agreement.

Waiver and Severability. The waiver of a breach of any provision of this Agreement shall not operate or be construed as a waiver of any other or subsequent breach. If any provision of this Agreement is held to be invalid, void or unenforceable, the remaining provisions shall nevertheless continue in full force and effect without being impaired or invalidated in any way.

Successors and Assigns. This Agreement will be binding upon my heirs, executors, administrators and other legal representatives and will be for the benefit of the Company Group, its successors, and its assigns. The Company may assign its rights and obligations under this Agreement to a third party.

Language. This Agreement may be written in the Chinese language and in the English language. In the event there is any conflict or inconsistency between the English version and the Chinese version of this Agreement, the English version shall prevail.

Application of this Agreement. I hereby agree that my obligations set forth in Sections 1 and 2 under this Agreement and the definitions of "Confidential Information" and "Inventions" contained therein shall be equally applicable to any work performed by me, and any Confidential Information and Inventions relating thereto, for the Company prior to the execution of this Agreement.

k. **Any other material contracts outstanding**

Need to make sure have revivified everything from each angle

CHAPTER SEVEN

Patent and Trademark Matters

Trademarks, patents, and trade secrets are all different types of intellectual property (IP). It is sometimes confusing to understand what exactly each type of IP protects. But understanding the differences between trademarks, patents, and trade secrets can help you understand how to best protect your works and enforce your rights.

A trademark is a word, phrase, symbol, and/or design that identifies and distinguishes the source of the goods of one party from those of others. A service mark is a word, phrase, symbol, and/or design that identifies and distinguishes the source of a service rather than goods. Examples include brand names, slogans, and logos. (The term "trademark" is often used in a general sense to refer to both trademarks and service marks.)

A patent protects inventions. These inventions can include new and useful processes, machines, manufactures, compositions of matter as well as improvements to them. The primary goal of the patent law is to encourage innovation and commercialization of technological advances. Patent law incentivizes inventors to publicly disclose their inventions in exchange for certain exclusive rights.

Trade secret protection protects secrets from unauthorized disclosure and use by others. A trade secret is information that has an economic benefit due to its secret nature, has value to others who cannot legitimately obtain it, and is subject to reasonable efforts to maintain its secrecy. The protections afforded by trade secret law are very different from others forms of IP.

Checklist

a. List of:

- All foreign and domestic patents and patent licenses held by the company
- Any trademarks, trade names or service marks
- Any copyrights

b. Copies of all material agreements for licensing of company technology to and from third parties.
c. Describe importance of existing patents and whether additional patents are necessary
d. Any correspondence from third parties regarding potential infringement of intellectual property right of others
e. List of proprietary processes controlled by the company
f. The contact and the name of the law firm which handles patent and trademark matters for the company

CHAPTER EIGHT

Manufacturing / Operational Aspects

There will be many aspects that affect the environmental performance of your business. Whether you work in manufacturing, services, or even the charity sector, many things that your staff do will have an environmental impact, even down to the decisions on how they travel to and from work, whether they use public transport – even the vehicles they choose to purchase for the commute to and from work. While we examined these in some detail in a previous blog post, we will now look specifically at the manufacturing process itself.

Grouping methodology: This method is just as the name suggests. You focus on one category at a time to identify aspects. Start with activities then move to products and finally, services. An activity, for instance, might be your fueling operation, and it may include several aspects, such as air emissions, chemical usage and spills. Each of these in turn has one or more impacts, from degradation of air quality to depletion of natural resources.

Surveying methodology: This approach revolves around geographic areas. Typically, you'll start at one end of your facility or site (property) and finish at the other end. It's a detailed walkthrough with a well-defined purpose. Try making a drawing of your facility (or working from an existing floor plan) and documenting the location of all aspects. Then log everything in detail in a simple spreadsheet along with corresponding impacts.

Mass balancing methodology: If you're an organization with an engineering mindset, the mass balancing or inputs and outputs methodology is probably a natural choice. It starts with all the inputs into your facility and finishes with the outputs. A short list of inputs might include people, equipment, chemicals, water and electricity. The corresponding outputs might be solid waste, fumes, widgets, wastewater, heat and radiation.

Back-calculating methodology: Is your organization more science-minded? Try working backwards. You know the potential answers, and they'll take you back to your aspects. Make a list of potential impacts (both negative and positive) your facility might have then work back to aspects. Sample impacts might be degradation of water quality or improvement of human health. Include both common and rare (emergency) impacts.

Potpourri methodology: It's a little bit of this and a little bit of that. The potpourri method generally combines two of the other methodologies. One common strategy is to combine grouping and surveying. You start at one end of the facility, focus on one area at a time and list out all activities, products and services. Then move to the next area and repeat. You're finished when you reach the other end of the site or facility.

Each of these methods has pros and cons, but with a little experimenting, you'll find the best match for your organization. Pick the method that sounds most appealing, gather a small group and start brainstorming.

a. **A breakdown by manufacturing/ service site of the products manufactured, personnel employed, number of shifts, and capacity**

- Make an extensive list of all "inputs" to your manufacturing process; these should include items as diverse as raw material, electricity and utility costs, packaging, travel costs, and anything else you deem has an environmental impact.
- Measure these accurately. Continual improvement is fundamental to the ISO 14001 standard, so having a firm grasp of your starting point is critical.
- Formulate a plan to remove or improve these aspects, including how and when they will be assessed, using the "Plan, Do, Check, Act" model, ensuring that your objectives and performance is correctly communicated and shared with your team.

a. **List of major suppliers and/or contract manufacturers or assemblers, showing total and type of purchases from each one during the last and current fiscal years (indicating which are sole suppliers)**

Need to check practices followed by company under any circumstances if they should not compromising basic purchase operating procedures

The four main types of purchases

Standard purchase: A standard purchase is typically used for irregular, infrequent or one-off procurement. As mentioned above, it contains a complete specification of the purchase, setting out the price, quantity and timeframes for payment and delivery. A restaurant might raise a standard purchase order when it purchases new tables and chairs. If all goes well, this should be a one-off purchase for the restaurant, and the contract will be fulfilled once the chairs are delivered in good order.

Planned purchase: Like a standard purchase, a planned purchase is relatively comprehensive. A planned purchase requires full details of the goods and services to be purchased and their costs. Dates for payment and delivery are also included in a planned purchase order, but these are treated as tentative dates. Issuing a release against the planned purchase order places individual orders. For example, a restaurant might require 500,000 disposable placemats in one year – the manager could create a planned purchase order with a commercial printer detailing the price and quantity with a tentative delivery schedule. After using the first 5,000 placemats, the restaurant would create a release against the purchase order to order more.

Blanket purchase: A blanket purchase involves a purchaser agreeing to purchase particular goods or services from a specific vendor, but not at any specific quantity. Pricing may or may not be confirmed in a blanket purchase order. This type of order is typically used for repetitive procurement of a specific set of items from a supplier such as basic materials and supplies. In the restaurant example above, they could equally choose to use a blanket purchase order to procure the disposable placemats — not having to confirm a specific quantity may make this a preferable option if the quantity required is not clear.

Contract purchase: A contract purchase sets out the vendor's details and potentially also payment and delivery terms. The products to be purchased are not specified. A contract purchase order is used to create an agreement and terms of supply between a purchaser and vendor as the basis for an ongoing commercial relationship. To order a product, the purchaser may refer to the contract purchase order when raising a standard purchase order.

c. **Material or outside of ordinary course of business contracts with suppliers, manufacturers, etc.**

Many M&A-agreements address the seller's or acquired companies' behaviour during certain periods of time. The transaction agreement either permits certain acts because they are in the ordinary course of business, warrants that various acts have been conducted in the ordinary course, or requires that an approval is obtained for certain acts outside the ordinary course. Accordingly, the purchaser would be protected against unusual acts or omissions affecting the acquired companies' business or intrinsic value, whilst the acquired companies are not burdened by unworkable approval requirements. For this purpose, the transaction agreement refers to the ordinary course of business, to acts consistent with past practice or wording importing the same concept.

In defining the ordinary course, it makes sense to start with what the Acquired Companies themselves believed was suitable in view of their size and the workability of what operational personnel and staff had always considered efficient. This suggests a reference to such acquired companies' or seller's internal approval policies, as well as to the normal operations and acts of purchase ordering. Alternatively, and in fact a strong argument for the purchaser during its negotiations, the SPA (sellers and Purchasers Agreement) could refer to the purchaser's approval policies.

A properly drafted set of internal approval policies should obviously divide what the various non-executive employees may or must do, from the unusual or significant acts that would require a decision from management. Because M&A (Mergers and acquisitions) transactions are sometimes stalled because a seller is fed up with the cowboy-type of behaviour of the companies to whom it sells, an objective standard should expressly set out the criteria of what is in the ordinary course of business.

Seller shall procure that pending Closing, Acquired Companies shall conduct business in all material respects only in the ordinary course of business.

Sellers shall not permit Acquired Companies to do any of the following pending the Closing without the prior written approval of Purchaser (which approval shall not be unreasonably withheld or delayed): ...

(A) Enter into an agreement or a series of related agreements that are not in the ordinary course of business, for an aggregate amount in excess of INR _____ ;

None of the Acquired Companies is a party to, or bound by: ...
(B) Any agreement or commitment relating to the disposition or acquisition of assets or any interest in any business enterprise outside the ordinary course of business.

An action taken by a company will be deemed to have been taken **in the ordinary course of business** only if:

(a) such action is consistent with the past practices of such company and is taken in the ordinary course of the normal day-to-day operations of such company;
(b) such action is not required to be authorised by the managing board or general meeting of shareholders of such company (or by any person or group of persons exercising similar authority) and is not required to be specifically authorised by an affiliate of such company; and
(c) such action is similar in nature, magnitude and frequency to actions customarily taken, without any authorisation by the managing board or general meeting of shareholders (or by any person or group of persons exercising similar authority), in the ordinary course of the normal day-to-day operations of other companies that are in the same line of business.

d. **Description of all toxic chemicals used in production and manner of storage and disposition**

Many agents/substances used or created at work could harm health. They include chemicals in all their forms, solid, liquid, gaseous including nanoparticles; as well as biological agents such as bacteria, viruses or other microorganisms, that can cause infection, an allergic reaction or are toxic. Biological risks also include the transmission of disease between humans or between animals and humans.

Employers should adequately control exposure to agents/substances, both chemical and biological, in the workplace that cause ill health. This means:

- identifying which harmful agents/substances may be present, used or generated, in the workplace;
- deciding how workers might be exposed to them and be harmed;
- looking at what measures they have in place to prevent this harm and deciding whether they are doing enough;
- providing information, instruction and training;

- In appropriate cases, providing health surveillance.

All elements of the control measures must be checked and reviewed regularly to make sure they continue to be effective. These checks should be adequate to determine whether improvements are required and will include:

- Maintaining plant and equipment – all ventilation equipment should be examined and tested regularly by a competent person (someone who has the necessary skills, knowledge and experience to carry out work safely). This may involve measuring the airflow or the pressures in the system, or air sampling in the workroom. In general, all extraction equipment must be examined and tested in accordance with national legislation;
- making sure systems of work are being followed and revising them if they are not working;
- Making sure personal protective equipment is suitable (offering effective protection against the identified hazard), used, properly fitted and (where appropriate) maintained.
- Making sure workers are properly vaccinated. Vaccination offers individual and collective protection.

Employers may need specialist advice, particularly for potentially serious risks or processes that are difficult to control, from someone who is competent in that area of work, e.g. an occupational hygienist.

e. Description of any EPA investigation and any other investigation or claim

Generally speaking, an environmental crime is a negligent, knowing or willful violation of a federal environmental law. "Knowing" violations are those that are deliberate and not the product of an accident or mistake. Environmental violations are not always obvious. Here are some signs of possible environmental violations.

- Strong, offensive, or unusual chemical odors
- Large numbers of dead birds, fish or other animals
- Pipes or valves appear hidden or bypass waste treatment systems
- Tank trucks discharging into drains, manholes or bodies of water

- Oily slicks on bodies of water
- Drums or containers dumped at odd hours in out-of-the way places
- Corroded, leaking waste containers

Typical violations:

- Illegal disposal of hazardous waste
- Export of hazardous waste without the permission of the receiving country
- Illegal discharge of pollutants to a water of the United States
- The removal and disposal of regulated asbestos containing materials in a manner inconsistent with the law and regulations
- Illegal importation of certain restricted or regulated chemicals into the United States
- Tampering with a drinking water supply
- Mail fraud/Wire fraud
- Conspiracy
- Money laundering relating to environmental criminal activities

Monitoring compliance includes more than inspecting facilities. The traditional inspection need to replace by advanced technologies and processes. Helps reduce costs and saves time and resources, while improving compliance and the accuracy of monitoring and reporting.

CHAPTER NINE

Operations

The aim of an operational audit is ultimately to optimize efficiency. By auditing the business's internal policies and procedures, the company can identify trouble spots and operate more effectively. The outcomes gleaned from the audit are most useful to the management team, who can take these recommendations on board to streamline future processes. Here are three of the primary outcomes of a successful operational audit:

1. Maximize efficiency: Gain a greater understanding of how future policies and procedures can boost effectiveness.
2. Understand risks: Businesses run many operational risks, ranging from health and safety issues to cyber threats. A full operational audit identifies risks like these, as well as potential problems related to fraud and compliance.
3. Finetune internal controls: By examining each step of the operational process, an audit can dive deeper into the impact of any changes to internal controls.

Operational audits can turn up unexpected problems that take time to repair. This might involve a complete overhaul of existing systems, requiring new training for employees. In the long run, these disruptions can be worth the trouble, should the operational audit lead to a more efficient method of doing business.

Checklist

a. List of third-party developers, software duplicators, and manual publishers showing total and type of project for each one during the last and current fiscal years (for third-party developments, include contact names, phone numbers, and forms of agreements)

b. Form of agreements relating to the sale or lease of material capital equipment
c. List of top 20 accounts payable with contact names and phone numbers
d. Checklist followed by company

CHAPTER TEN

Sales and Marketing

It's important to consider undertaking a Sales & marketing audit in order to identify and review the current status of a company's Sales & marketing activities and help reduce future costs. Particularly for small to medium sized businesses that are wanting to find out what activities are working and what activities are not working as well and measuring this against expenditure and then overall ROI, the sales & marketing audit becomes a must-have part of the entire process. A comprehensive review of a company's sales & marketing and communication really helps a business understand where it's heading from a marketing perspective. By reviewing issues such as: customers and your target audience; your competitors; the market place in general and your internal situation; you will be more informed about the success of previous marketing activities. A marketing audit analyses the business objectives and understands what it is the business is trying to achieve providing leaders with the opportunity to make more informed decisions on their future marketing direction. The information is also invaluable in helping businesses build a successful marketing strategy and highlights what they will need to deliver the most cost effective marketing strategy in order to meet their business objectives.

How does a sales & marketing audit help a business meet its goals?

A thorough marketing audit provides a benchmark for monitoring future marketing activity and highlights recommendations to improve the efficiency and performance of your company's marketing activity. A sales & marketing audit is often used by a company reviewing its business strategy. A marketing audit can inform management with an invaluable customer and market insight, vital to help them set realistic business objectives.

Key elements that may be covered in a sales & marketing audit should include:

- **The SWOT analysis**
- **Customer and prospect research**
- **Competitor landscape analysis**
- **Review of current internal marketing activities assessing their impact and results in the past and:-**
- **Overview of external market factors covering the PESTLE analysis**

More importantly look at all the aspects of your business from a marketing perspective including the following key elements:-

- What resources does your company have for marketing & sales? This includes resources both internal and external?
- What type of marketing material, brochures and flyers do you use to promote your company to prospects? How do you use it? How often?
- What promotional vehicles do you utilise including website, collateral, direct marketing, interactive and online marketing?
- What about event vehicles such as trade shows, special events, seminars and webinars
- What is the state of your technological and analytical vehicles used for marketing purposes – including database, market research and CRM systems? How could they be used more efficiently and integrated so they provide a 360-degree view of your customer?
- What is your website like and how is it being used? In addition, what do the statistics for website performance look like?
- What social media channels is your business using and how engaged are you currently with your followers across the various platforms?
- What do your customers and prospects think of your company? How do they engage with your organisation and at what level?
- What about the overall customer experience you provide– what is the customer experience at various touch points of your organisation

External factors are equally as important when undertaking a comprehensive marketing audit. It is important to recognise that although we may have no control over external factors they are still hugely influential and therefore very important to consider when setting your business and marketing objectives.

Checklist and Reports to Check

a. Copies of all market research and/or marketing studies conducted in the last three years
b. List of the company's products, services, and competitors
c. List of the company's 20 largest customers or groups in each of the last two fiscal years, including contact name and phone number for each customer and indicating the types of products and the amounts of each purchased
d. All material licensing agreements, franchises, and conditional sales contracts to which the company is a party
e. Agreements with distributors, VAR's, OEMs, dealers, and sales representatives.
f. Copies of long-term sales contracts
g. Sales qualified leads (SQLs) Analysis
h. Marketing qualified leads (MQLs) Analysis
a. Customer Acquisition Cost Analysis
j. Customer Retention Analysis
k. Copies of competition analysis
ax. Copies of new competitors research analysis
all. Copies of product positioning analysis
n. Company-financed customer purchase agreements
o. Service and support contracts and marketing agreements
p. All material agency and advertising contracts to which the company is a party
q. Forms of warranties and guarantees provided to customers
r. Copies of all sales literature and forms
s. List of top 20 accounts receivable with contact names and phone numbers
t. Backlog at end of the most recent fiscal year and most recent fiscal quarter

CHAPTER ELEVEN

Tangible Property

a. List of real and material personal property owned by the company and documents of title, mortgages, deeds of trust, and security agreements pertaining to the properties
b. All outstanding leases for real and personal property to which the Company is either a lessor or lessee
c. List of any security interests in personal property
d. Documentation of significant acquisitions or dispositions of assets

CHAPTER TWELVE

Litigation and Audits

Get written assurances from management as to the completeness of the accounting for and disclosure of litigation, claims, and assessments in the financial statements. Examine invoices from lawyers and the legal expenses ledger account during and after the period being audited.

The advantage of a legal audit, though, is that it gives the opportunity to allow someone else to take a dispassionate, informed, look inside, which can be immensely valuable. It can allow you to talk about legal risk, controls and resourcing with the organisation from a position of strength. It can identify opportunities to integrate yourselves with the organisation, to build stronger internal relationships, and showcase the value of your internal specialisms.

Company need to Avoid Licensure Penalties, Fees, and Fines: Running a business in any municipality requires you to meet specific licensing, certification, and permit requirements. These laws change frequently, and it's easy to miss a new requirement if you're caught up in the day-to-day work of running a company. Failing to apply for or renew a license in a timely manner can lead to costly fees and penalties that cut into your profits and can even halt business operations.

Contracts should be in Order: Contracts are a crucial part of your business. A careful legal audit ensures that all of your contracts utilize the appropriate language, protect your business assets, and meet legal requirements. During a legal audit, you can get advice on missing, inaccurate, or unclear portions of contracts and decide which changes you want to make. If a dispute occurs between your company and a client, investor, or supplier, you can rest easy knowing that your contracts protect your company's rights and best interests.

Organisations to Avoid Employee Issues and Strengthen Morale: As a business owner, you rely heavily on your team to help you meet goals and keep clients happy. During a legal audit, your attorney can help you avoid common personnel issues and problems. They may look at your application process, verify that employee handbooks have all the necessary and required information, and review employment policies to ensure they are compliant with local and federal law. Additionally, a legal audit may identify potential areas of conflict between the company and its employees, giving you the chance to come up with policies and procedures that protect your business from potential liabilities.

Having Transparency to Investors and Consumers: Transparency is an essential component of business in today's world. A legal audit offers an impartial look at your company's operations and legal procedures, providing objective advice that can keep your business safe from litigation. The results of a legal audit send a strong message to those who work for or with your company, showing them that you have nothing to hide. This can be exceptionally helpful during a period of major growth when you are trying to draw in new investors, clients, or partners.

Auditing standards require an auditor to make various enquiries about liabilities in general

this may entail consideration of potential litigations and claims that the audited entity may be

facing. To perform this part of audit, the auditors will generally seek representation letters

from lawyers of the company detailing an estimate prepared by management, confirmed by

their lawyers through a representation letter, and then sent directly to the auditors

Auditing standards require an auditor to make various enquiries about liabilities in general

this may entail consideration of potential litigations and claims that the audited entity may be

facing. To perform this part of audit, the auditors will generally seek representation letters

from lawyers of the company detailing an estimate prepared by management, confirmed by

their lawyers through a representation letter, and then sent directly to the auditors.

Areas of audit might include:

- **Organisational structure** – the constitutional documentation of the organisation and its subsidiaries; whether they reflect current good practice; whether reporting, the appointment of directors and secretaries (if used) are up-to-date; whether there are any issues of concern on the public register.
- **Ownership documentation of organisational property and assets** – is it in order? Are there gaps or risks? Does the organisation have a system in place to track expiry and renewal dates, for example for leases?
- **Contractual arrangements** – these will differ for various types of organisation – more complex and detailed for a contractor than for an organisation which simply provides services, for example – but should include sale and purchase documentation, key contracts, documentation and agreements.
- **Litigation and disputes** – both present, possible, and (if any) past, whether they impact current arrangements in any way.
- **Intellectual property** – trademarks, patents and other intellectual property rights and licenses.
- **Formal operating** agreements, joint ventures and shareholder agreements for associated organisations.
- **Human resources** policies and procedures, including employee contracts, handbooks and any trade union agreements
- **Risk transfer** arrangements such as limitation of liability, insurance and third-party risk transfer agreements.

Checklist

a. All letters which have been sent to auditors in connection with year-end and current interim audits
b. Copies of any auditor letters to management regarding internal accounting controls
c. Descriptions of (and reasons for) any change in accounting methods in the past three years
d. Active litigation files
e. Any litigation settlement documents
f. Any decrees, orders, or judgments of courts or governmental agencies
g. Description of any warranty claims which have been made against the company, any subsidiary, or any partnership/joint venture and

the resolution of such claim

h. Information regarding any material litigation to which the company is a party or in which it may become involved

CHAPTER THIRTEEN

Environmental

Each property that is owned by the company should have an environmental audit performed. The action may be accomplished after a list of land and structures has been collated. Then, each property may be crossed from the list systematically. An itemized catalog should also list every hazardous substance that is used by the company for operations. If no activities have been completed on the land, then any contaminants discovered are due to the current company's practices. To reveal other environmental dangers, the potential buyer should obtain a list of all permits, licenses and similar items to compare what environmental risks may exist. Documentation sent and received from the company to the Environmental Protection Agency, state and local agencies may also reveal similar contaminants that have been used or leaked on the land. Legal assistance may discover litigation or investigations with the company for these risks and dangers due to chemicals, substances and gases. Exposure to employees and internal hazards should be filed in paperwork for an expert to learn. Some unrelated processes such as taxes and book keeping could reveal other sources of contaminants. With a full survey and assessment of the company and property, it may be possible to find all resources, materials and equipment that has harmed the environment.

Checklist

a. Schedule of hazardous materials stored, manufactured, or located at any facility of the company either now or in the past, or that the company ships or transports (hazardous materials means any substance or any material containing a substance that could be considered toxic or hazardous under Federal or state law)
b. Schedule of:

- Chemicals, toxic substances, or air contaminants which are regulated by Government Authorities present in any facility of the company
- Any incidents involving the release of a potentially hazardous amount of any carcinogen into, or presence of asbestos in, the workplace
- All instances in the past in which the company has corrected unsafe working conditions
- All the facilities of the company that discharge waste into any body of water, stream, or any sanitation system
- All permits or approvals obtained from any governmental body responsible for environmental or health regulation
- All occasions in which a liquid or solid waste material or any fuel or other hazardous material was accidentally or intentionally spilled or released

c. Any notices of violation or requests for information that have been received or threatened at any time for alleged failure of any facility to comply with applicable air pollution laws or with any air quality permit

CHAPTER FOURTEEN

Employees

Managing the employees in your workplace effectively necessitates that even the smallest of businesses set up work rules. Work rules protect your business and your workers, and if correctly implemented and executed, they create and maintain a better work environment for all. Having formal work rules in your business, even if they're not required, are a good idea because they can help you protect your business from potential liability and maintain a high quality of work life for your employees. It's also a good idea to make sure that your employees understand what is expected of them, not only in the work that they do, but in their behavior and in other areas of your employment relationship. If the rules are carefully selected, clearly related to the business, and fairly enforced, they can help you to better manage your workplace and your workers.

One of the most persuasive reasons for having a set of solid work rules is that they can protect your business. Many employers have rules because having them may help protect them from liability both legal and financial and give them more freedom in managing and disciplining employees. Evidence of the work rules and policies that were in place are often introduced by employers in cases where employees make employment-related claims such as wrongful discharge or discrimination claims.

When you terminate an employee you want your reasoning and your actions to be sound and defensible. It is helpful if you had clearly stated work rules that have been communicated to your employees. Then, an employee who breaks a work rule does so with the knowledge that the conduct is unacceptable and that such behavior might result in termination. Another benefit of having clear work rules is that it helps ensure that your employees understand what acceptable behavior is and what isn't. A clear definition of what is required and the consequences of failing to comply make it easier for you to respond consistently to work rule violations. An ambiguous rule or uneven enforcement of any rule opens your actions to challenge as arbitrary or discriminatory.

Work rules can help improve quality of work life by:

- Creating an atmosphere where employees are treated with dignity and respect
- Helping to ensure that employees conduct themselves in a professional and safe manner
- Encouraging open communication between you and your employees
- Ensuring that all employees are treated fairly and that they follow the same rules

Checklist

a. Description of any significant labor problems or union activities the company has experienced
b. Number of employees, broken down by major types of employees and a management organization chart
c. Resumés of key employees.
d. Contractual and discretionary bonuses and/or benefits details
e. The Company's personnel handbook and a schedule of all employee benefits and holiday, vacation, and sick leave policies.
f. A description of all employee problems within the last three years, including alleged wrongful termination, harassment, and discrimination.
g. A description of any labor disputes, requests for arbitration, or grievance procedures currently pending or settled within the last three years.
a. A list and description of benefits of all employee health and welfare insurance policies or self-funded arrangements.

CHAPTER FIFTEEN

Management

To evaluate the management team in its effectiveness to work in the interests of shareholders, maintain good relations with employees, and uphold reputational standards. It is important to stress that the management audit assesses the overall management of the company, not the performance of individual managers.

The goal of a management audit is to identify the weaknesses of the management team. The audit is most often carried out on a companywide basis but it can also be isolated to certain business segments. The goal is always to find out how effective management is and where it can improve. Areas that a management audit will cover but are not limited to include human resources, marketing, research and development (R&D), budgeting, operations, finance, information systems, and corporate structure. The management audit will consist of interviews with management and employees, an analysis of financial statements and performance, a study of a company's policies and procedures, an evaluation of training programs, the hiring process, and many other areas within an organization. When the audit is complete, the external audit company will not only provide its findings but will most often provide an entire plan for the board of directors to implement so that the company can operate at an optimal level.

A management audit might address such questions as the following:

- What organizational structure has been set up by management? Are there clear lines of reporting or is there confusion?
- What are the policies and procedures of the finance group, and is it always in compliance?
- How effective are current risk management measures?
- What is the state of relations among the employees of the organization?
- How does management put together its annual budget?

- Are the company's IT systems kept up-to-date?
- Is the management group responsive to shareholders?
- How effective is workforce recruitment and retention? Are there training programs to keep skills current among employees?
- Is management doing its job to ensure the company is a "good corporate citizen"?
- Is management strategically guiding the company toward its financial targets?

Checklist of Audit

a. Completed copies of Directors' and Officers' Questionnaires
b. Detailed resume of directors and top management personnel
c. Founders' agreements, management employment agreements, indemnification agreements, and "golden parachute" agreements
d. Schedule of all compensation paid in the most recent fiscal year to officers, directors, and key employees (separately showing salary, bonuses, and non-cash compensation)
e. Bonus plans, retirement plans, pension plans, deferred compensation plans, profit sharing, and management incentive agreements
f. Agreements for loans to and any other agreements with officers or directors
g. Description of any transactions between the company and any insider

CHAPTER SIXTEEN

Other Review

a. **Copy of any internal or outside studies of the company or the market for its products**

Research is an important element in a company when wanting to understand consumer behavior, demographics, and experimenting new products or services. This can be done through different types of strategies such as surveys, focus groups, and observations. They both have their advantages, but it's up to the firms to decide which option they will use to gather data. Now, the company should closely consider the advantages of each marketing research method and further analyze the disadvantages as well. Overall, external and internal marketing research is an important aspect when gathering data or beginning a project.

a. **Summary of all Legal inquiries**

Many a times companies are incorporated for carrying out of acts which may not necessarily be legal in the strictest sense or for evading liabilities and responsibility under a certain legislation. These activities impact the other members such as creditors, depositors and the financial system in general. There is clear and a close relationship between corporate governance and ethics but conflicts between the two are certain. Such conflicts if not taken care of reduce the confidence of potential investors and affect the global credibility of the Government. Keeping the same in mind, the law on inspection, inquiry and investigation of companies has been tightened. The main objective of an investigation is a form of deeper probe into the affairs of a company. It is a fact-finding exercise to collect evidence and to see if any illegal acts or offences are disclosed and then decide the action to be taken.

Following the Closing, Seller will handle and process all civil and criminal subpoenas, summons, court-ordered or government or agency or regulatory demands for documents and all similar legal notices or other information, and all notices, claims, demands of any kind from customers or third parties (collectively, "Subpoenas") served on Seller prior to the Closing Date that relate to the Acquired Assets or the Deposits.

c. **Summary of State, local, and foreign income tax status**

To check all taxation filings before taking over business because Taxation is used primarily to raise revenue for government expenditures, though it can serve other purposes as well. They are not going to leave you if any taxation is pending

d. **Permits for conduct of business**

Regulations are also constantly changing. Each year, license registration requirements change, and enforcement actions against business license violations are increasing. Changes to your business operations, locations, or offerings can also trigger new requirements. If your company is not compliant, it could face penalties, fines, interruption to business growth, and adverse publicity.

- Document your existing license portfolio and licensing footprint
- Create a list of all the information that must be reported on each filing
- Compare this list to your portfolio footprint and document potential gaps.

e. **A schedule of all pending litigation.**

With respect to a list prepared by management, an identification of the omission of any pending or threatened litigation, claims, and assessments

f. **A description of any threatened litigation.**

An organization that is contemplating acquiring a target that is the subject of pending or threatened litigation should, among other items, address the following high-level considerations:

- **Due Diligence:** Purchasers should involve litigation counsel at the outset of the due diligence process to understand and evaluate the costs, risks and likely outcomes of the litigation, as well as develop strategies to address those risks and engage with the target.
- **Negotiate the Costs of the Claim:** Informed by the due diligence process, the parties may discuss which party will assume costs of the claim if judgment against the target is awarded. A purchaser may discount the purchase price by the quantum (if known) of the claim, or saddle the vendor with ongoing liability for the claim by way of specific indemnity.
- **Negotiate Control of the Defense:** If the claims are fundamental to the purchased business, the purchaser will likely wish to maintain full control of the defense strategy in order to protect its acquisition. If the target is assuming control of the defense, the purchaser must stipulate that any settlement or admission of responsibility requires its consent or else it risks outcomes that may not be in its best interest.
- **Representations, Warranties and Indemnification:** The purchaser must have sufficient assurances that the information that it has received from the target regarding the pending or threatened litigation is accurate in order to properly structure the litigation risks into the transaction. The target's indemnification of the purchaser should, as specifically as possible, reflect the litigation risks identified in the due diligence in order to sufficiently protect the purchaser. Purchasers may also consider withholding a portion of the purchase price, subject to certain litigation outcomes, for additional protection.
- **Asset Purchase:** If the litigation risks are too great for the purchaser, it may consider buying the assets of the business rather than the shares/units/interests of the target, and leave some or all of the liabilities behind with the target. However, purchasers should be aware that some liabilities, such as environmental liabilities, may follow the related assets without a specific assumption in the asset purchase agreement.

Each transaction will always have its own unique circumstances

g. **Copies of insurance policies possibly providing coverage as to pending or threatened litigation.**

There are many types of **business insurance**. General liability, commercial property, business income and workers' compensation are just a few types

1. Liability Insurance Policies

- A Liability Insurance is there to help protect you against any claims resulting from damage or injury that may be caused by your business's operations, its products, or on its premises. There are many types of liability insurance:
- General Liability Insurance - A type of insurance coverage that businesses need to protect themselves against any legal liability for damages or injuries to any third party, plus advertising injuries and personal injuries as well as any injuries or damages that take place because of your business's operations.
- **Public Liability Insurance** - Covers you and your business against any damages or losses caused to a third-party (i.e., anyone other than you—the insured person or business—and the insurance company) on the premises.
- **Professional Liability Insurance** - Protects you or your business against claims of professional negligence, errors, or omissions. It is most useful for professionals like architects, engineers, consultants, lawyers, building designers, medical professionals, and accountants.
- Management Liability - This insurance is there to protect your company's directors and officers against circumstances that aren't usually covered under a public or general liability policy, like allegations of wrongdoing, directed at the company's managers, directors and officers.
- **Contractual Liability** - This covers you and your business against contractual liabilities, or those liabilities that you and your business would assume from entering into a contract of any nature, like a lease, rental agreement, or other common business contracts. It will cover you for things like financial losses and legal expenses.

2. Property Insurance Policies

- Property Insurance covers you in case of any loss damage, or theft to your commercial property, and its contents, whether it is a personal or rented business space.

- **Building Insurance** - A building insurance plan insures shops, buildings, offices, and other commercial properties from fires, natural calamities, burglaries, and a number of other damage to buildings.
- **Consequential Loss (Fire) Insurance** - A fire insurance covers expenses incurred due to consequential damages of property due to fire breakouts. So, if your shop is damaged by a fire, it will help you cover for any loss to your business and revenue that you might face because of the damage to your shop. *Disclaimer - Fire Insurance is not a standalone product. To avail this cover, you need to purchase Digit's SFSP policy with a Fire cover add-on.
- Sign Board Insurance - This covers your business against any accidental loss or damage to the signboards and hoardings that are placed outside and in public from dangers like natural perils, fire, and theft. It also covers against legal liability in case the signboard is the cause of any third-party damages.
- Plate Glass Insurance - A type of insurance policy that will protect your business against any damage or breakage of large panes of glass on your commercial buildings, like shop windows, glass doors, transparent walls, and more.
- **Burglary Insurance** - This burglary insurance policy covers you in case of theft of cash, jewellery and other valuable products, as well as any losses and damages that can be caused due to a burglary. *Disclaimer - Burglary Insurance is not a standalone product. To avail this cover, you need to purchase Digit's SFSP policy with a Burglary add-on.

3. Money Insurance

- It is there to help you protect your business's money and monetary transactions, including cash, cheques, drafts, postal orders. You and your business will be protected in case of theft, loss, or accidental damage to your money, while it is in transit or secured in a safe or cash counter.

4. Fidelity Guarantee Insurance

- This protects you and your business against any loss directly resulting from the dishonest acts of your employees during the course of their employment. So, a fidelity insurance will protect your business from any financial costs incurred as a result of dishonesty, theft or fraudulent acts by employees.

5. Electronic Equipment Insurance

- This will protect you in case your business's electronic equipment faces any loss or material damage to electronic equipment (which can include systems software). This includes costs of repair or replacement, loss or damage to any external data, and the increased cost of working when your equipment is out of commission.

6. Commercial Vehicle Insurance

- A Commercial Vehicle Insurance policy will cover damages and losses caused to or by a commercial vehicle and its owner-driver in situations like accidents, collisions, natural calamities, fires, etc.
- If your business owns one or many vehicles, or involves the use of vehicles, such as cabs, this coverage is essential. This type of insurance covers passenger carrying vehicles (like cabs, autos, buses, etc.), goods carrying vehicles (like trucks, tempos, lorries, etc.) and any special vehicles used for farming, mining or construction.
- It is mandatory for all businesses to buy a commercial vehicle insurance for their vehicles, such as for auto-rickshaws, cabs, school buses, tractors, commercial vans and trucks, amongst others.

7. Worker's Compensation Insurance

- This policy is for employers when they provide compensation to their employees in case of accidents that happen while they are on the job. It covers employees in the case of diseases, bodily injury, disability, or death caused due to accidents in course of employment and helps them to get the care they need.
- By doing this, it enables employers to meet the requirements of the Workmen Compensation Act and protection from lawsuits.

8. Group Health Insurance Policies

- **Employee Health Insurance** - An Employee Health Insurance is a health insurance plan that covers the employees of an organization, under one policy, where the premium is borne by the employer. The price for the same is comparatively a lot less as compared to individual health insurance plans and, it also benefits employers in tax reductions, therefore making it beneficial for both the employer and employee.

- **Group COVID–19 Cover** - COVID-19 Group Protection is a health insurance policy that is designed to cover employees during the coronavirus pandemic. It provides coverage for any medical expenses that they may have during treatment for COVID-19.

h. **Documents relating to any injunctions, consent decrees, or settlements to which the Company is a party.**

To check all documents related to injunctions or settlements

i. **A list of unsatisfied judgments.**

List of judgments that have been legally made against a person or company but have not paid.

j. **A schedule of all law firms, accounting firms, consulting firms, and similar professionals engaged by the Company during past five years.**

Last Five Year calendar of all third party audit firms with audit report

k. **Copies of all articles and press releases relating to the Company within the past three years.**

Need to audit to analyse if any misleading information published

ax. **Equity Management**

Equity management is the process of creating and managing owners in your company. This may sound simple, but it involves everything from tracking and reporting changes in ownership to updating documents, communicating with stakeholders, consulting your board of directors, and staying compliant. One of the objectives of equity management is to draw new members to the organization along with satisfying the current employees. While adhering to all the principles, equity management has to allow growth while maintaining cooperative profitability.

Typically, equity is referred to as owner's equity or shareholder's equity. In the case where the company has to be liquidated, after the sale of all the assets and debt paid off, equity refers to the amount of money the company shareholders will receive. Additionally, shareholder's equity can also represent the company's book value and the pro-rata ownership of the company's shares. Being one of the essentials to assess the financial health of the company, equity is a common piece of information that is employed by analysts. It can be found on the balance sheet of the company's financial records.

all. **Elements to be incorporated into merger agreement:**

- Assign responsibility to the acquiring or to-be acquired firm during the interim period for damage or loss of property being conveyed, or for claims arising out of the acquisition.
- Require that the acquired firm keep all insurance policies in force until notified otherwise.
- Stipulate that a broad-form named insured clause be added for the newly merged or acquired entities.
- Specify that any insurance policies of the acquired firm that come up for renewal during the interim period will be reviewed by the acquiring company before renewal.
- If the acquisition is by purchase of assets, specify that the insurance policies of the selling company are not a part of the assets to be purchased. The acquired company does not immediately cease to exist. It lives until all assets have been distributed and dissolution is accomplished. It continues to have employees, and can be sued even if it has no other assets than proceeds of sale. Even after dissolution, distributed assets can be legally attached for some period of time.
- If continuation of insurance is desired, i.e., property or auto, contact the broker or carrier and have new policies issued effective at the time of the transfer of title of the assets. All cancellations, audits, etc., relating to the policies owned by the selling company then become the responsibility of the seller rather than the buyer.
- Stipulate, if possible, that the seller continue liability insurance for a number of years after the date of sale, particularly if claim-sensitive

products are involved. It is not unusual to require the selling company to continue coverage in force beyond the date of sale in order to cover any occurrences relating to products manufactured prior to a merger. WATCH OUT FOR CLAIMS MADE POLICIES!

- Avoid coverage gaps by providing special wording in the purchase contract so that the acquiring firm has the benefit of the acquired company's insurance. This is crucial for any claims based on occurrences prior to the date of acquisition -- it is highly unlikely that the liability carrier of the acquiring company would cover such claims. With recent successor liability decisions, this is becoming more and more important.
- Assign respective responsibilities for liability that may arise or be discovered after the signing of the contract (inadequate insurance, retroactive coverage, product recall, etc.).

n. **Items to consider:**

- Review coverages in effect.
- Where products are involved, identify product lines, including old and discontinued products that may give rise to claims. Review old annual reports, 10Ks, and other documents.
- Evaluate exposure to product liability claims under successor liability rules. Assess ways of minimizing exposures.
- Evaluate loss experience. Determine impact on future premium costs. Pay particular attention to products, workers' compensation, and professional liability claims that could have long payout periods. Review reserves to see if "sleepers" exist which could result in major judgments. Estimate an IBNR figure.
- Verify open claims for sufficiency of coverage and evaluation of deductibles or SIR's.
- What are total insurance costs? Will they be higher or lower after acquisition?
- Evaluate exposure to asbestos and pollution claims, including claims that may arise from discontinued operations. Assess methods of minimizing exposures.

◦ **SUCCESSOR LIABILITY**

- Background: A defunct firm's liability used to be limited, but this is changing. Today, a company may be held liable for the products of a firm acquired twenty or thirty years ago and long defunct.

  Most states have specific common law rules on successor liability; these rules are broadening on a case-by-case basis
- Steps to take: Weigh products liability exposure of the acquired firm in light of recent court decisions. If exposure exits, consider the following action:

  - Change the product as well as personnel and management of the acquired firm, and if possible, the physical location.
  - Buy assets rather than company stock and dissolve the firm.
  - Contractually express refusal of accepting liability for the acquired firm's previous deeds in order to avoid implied acceptance.
  - Make it clear to everyone that the old firm no longer exists, and that you do not provide services for the predecessor's products. Do not take over existing service contracts.
  - Add an indemnification clause to the contract of purchase that the acquiring firm will be held harmless.

The need for and availability of successor liability insurance should be determined. Such insurance will not avoid liability but it will help defray legal and claims costs if liability were imposed. Take care that such a policy expressly covers liability for the defunct firm's products without limitation as to the date of manufacture.

p. <u>After Merger is completed</u>

1. After the merger is accomplished, financial priorities may have shifted, working capital may be strained, and therefore, levels of self-assumption of risk may need to be lowered. On the other hand, the larger financial structure may call for higher retentions.

2. Accumulation of values may need reevaluation, as do the extra expense and business interruption exposures, particularly, if a close interdependence of operations between the acquired and acquiring firm is expected.

3. Policies may need to be brought back into the risk manager's file so that he or she is prepared for divestitures and spin-offs. Some of the subsidiaries or plants of the acquired firms may not fit into the corporate plan, and, by being spun off, ease the corporate debt burden.

4. Final success from the standpoint of the risk manager means the following:

- A well conceived and effective program of communications to assure smooth cooperation between the risk manager and the personnel of the acquired firm. The basis will be a redrawn corporate policy and risk management manual.
- Appropriate and well understood claims procedures.
- Active liaison between the acquiring firm's brokers and insurance carriers and the acquired firm.

A great deal of tact to achieve active cooperation rather than resigned acceptance throughout all phases of the acquisition period.

www.ingramcontent.com/pod-product-compliance
Ingram Content Group UK Ltd.
Pitfield, Milton Keynes, MK11 3LW, UK
UKHW022015190726
13853UKWH00005B/1954